**SCHOLASTIC**

*Forestell*

# Leveled Reading-Response Activities for Guided Reading

## 70+ Comprehension-Boosting Reproducibles That Provide Just-Right Activities for Readers at Every Level From A to N

### by Rhonda Graff

New York ○ Toronto ○ London ○ Auckland ○ Sydney
New Delhi ○ Mexico City ○ Hong Kong ○ Buenos Aires

**Teaching** *Resources*

# Dedication

*To my parents, Craig, Daniel,*
*Holly, Lori, and Tony,*
*and a special thank you to*
*Karen Kellaher, Liza Charlesworth,*
*and Jaime Lucero at Scholastic*

Edited by Karen Kellaher
Cover and interior design by Grafica
Illustrations by Jaime Lucero and Teresa Anderko

ISBN: 978-0-545-44271-8

# CONTENTS

# Introduction

If you use guided reading in a primary classroom, you already know the great advantages this type of small-group instruction can offer. Whether you use the approach exactly as it was outlined by Irene Fountas and Gay Su Pinnell in the 1990s or have adapted the idea to your specific classroom needs, you've undoubtedly seen benefits: By focusing your attention on a handful of students with similar abilities and needs, you can provide plenty of individualized support and carefully monitor each reader's growth. You can select texts that are appropriate for each reading stage and identify the specific strategies—such as rereading or visualization—that will help those particular students make sense of the text when they encounter difficulties.

But you may also have faced a logistical conundrum: What on earth do you do with the other 15 or more students in the class while you work with one small group at a time? I've used small-group instruction throughout my teaching career, and I admit it took me a while to figure this one out! Even today, there are days that do not go according to plan, especially when I am dealing with a large class or outside distractions. The goal is to keep the other students engaged in developmentally appropriate activities, allowing them to apply and practice the skills and strategies they've learned through the year. The activity should be something they can tackle after receiving direct instruction and a clear explanation by the teacher. It must be interesting and student-friendly, since you need them to stay on task for a set period of time. That's where you can implement the reading-response activities in this book.

I created this volume of reproducible activities to serve as opportunities for students to interact with fiction texts and practice the skills and concepts they have been taught during reading lessons and in small reading groups. While you are working with one reading group, your other students can use the reproducibles to boost comprehension and reinforce and extend their thinking. Although some actives may be compatible with nonfiction texts, this volume is primarily focused on fiction.

## Understanding the Levels

The activities are labeled with alphabetic levels that correspond to the levels traditionally used in guided reading. If you are unfamiliar with these levels, the chart below illustrates how the levels typically match up to primary grade levels. Of course, this is just a very rough guide; you may have first graders enthusiastically and fluently reading the Junie B. Jones series (leveled M) or second graders starting school at a C or D level, especially if they are learning English as a second language. The levels seen in a particular grade level can also vary considerably from district to district.

Deciding what level a student is reading at involves observation and assessment, and there are many tools available,

| GRADE: | Guided reading levels you may see: |
| --- | --- |
| Kindergarten | A, B, C, D |
| 1 | A, B, C, D, E, F, G, H, I |
| 2 | E, F, G, H, I, J, K, L, M, N |

both in print and online, to assist you with this. (For a list of guided reading resources from Scholastic, see page 175.) You can easily assess the levels of books in your classroom library using online resources, including Scholastic's web site (www.scholastic.com). Once you know at what level each student is reading, you can select the set of reproducible activities in this book that will work best for him or her. Keep in mind that students in the primary grades can progress quickly, so it's a good idea to informally reassess as often as needed.

The levels in this book have been paired (A/B, C/D, and so on) for the sake of organization and simplicity. For each paired level, there are ten reproducible activities, along with teacher notes and tips for each one. You will notice overlapping objectives; many of the targeted skills and concepts (such as characters, setting and story events, or words with multiple meanings) appear in several levels throughout the book. As the levels increase, the skill or concept is presented with increasing task complexity.

These overlapping skills correspond to the overlapping grade-level objectives in the Common Core State Standards, on which this book is based. These standards set a high bar for what students should be able to do as they interact with text. For a complete list of the Common Core standards addressed, see pages 172–173.

When you are choosing the activities you will distribute to students, I encourage you to think flexibly about the levels. The fact that a student is reading at level K does not necessarily mean that he or she cannot do an M/N activity. While each activity was created with students at a specific level in mind, most can be used across several levels. You may find that you love an activity that is a level or two away from where your students are reading. Preview it and give it a try; you may very well find that it is something that your students can handle. Also note that many of the activities at levels A/B and C/D do not have writing lines. At these early literacy levels, many students have not yet received formal handwriting instruction or they may not yet have the fine motor control needed. Also, students at the early reading levels are not independent, so they will need guidance even when the activities are familiar.

## Choosing Books

The majority of the reproducibles in this volume call on students to interact with a single fiction book—for example, by identifying story elements, describing the author's message, or giving an opinion about the text. How that fiction book gets selected is entirely up to you. You may ask students to respond to a leveled book that you read and discussed in an instructional guided reading group the previous day. Alternatively, you may choose a different book for students to read for the purposes of the activity. You may even allow students to select new books on their own from the classroom's leveled library. Selecting one's own books for independent reading is an essential element in a successful guided reading classroom, but you'll need to double check that students are selecting books they can both decode and comprehend successfully. Although the goal of these activities is independent practice, it is key that children have feedback as soon as possible and redirection as needed.

There are many wonderful books out there that will work perfectly for these activities. When I am selecting titles, I look for books that are interesting and can lend themselves to good teaching opportunities. When children have trouble decoding, I make sure I use materials to address their specific learning needs. Controlled readers (books that use tightly controlled text) can be valuable tools for some students. However, controlled readers tend to have limited storylines and character development and are not easily leveled. Therefore, if using controlled readers, be sure to choose reproducibles that align with the text.

While the reproducible activities you'll find here are largely designed for use with fiction, don't be afraid to use an activity in conjunction with a nonfiction book if it seems to be a good fit. This is especially true for activities that ask students to list details from the text, work with vocabulary, or make observations about illustrations or photographs.

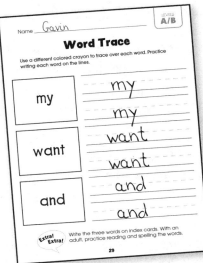

## Using the Reproducibles

Because every classroom is unique, the activities at each level in this book are designed to be flexible. You may use them in any order you like. You may have all of the students at a particular level work on the same page at the same time, or make copies of several reproducibles available at a literacy station and allow each student to select one. Because many skills and concepts spiral throughout the levels, you may choose one concept (setting, for example) and have all of your non-instructional groups work on level-appropriate versions of the same concept at the same time. However you use them, I offer these tips:

- **Preview the reproducibles before making your copies.** A number of the reproducibles require teacher input prior to reproduction. For example, a page might ask you to preselect vocabulary words from the text. As you can imagine, it's much easier to write these specifics on the page before making your class copies. These "blank slate" pages are among my favorites, and I think they will be among yours as well; they allow you to really focus on what's important and appropriate for your classroom and your curriculum. This step is **crucial**!

- **Use the teacher notes.** The notes for each reproducible alert you if there's anything special you should do or review before students complete the page. While many of the activities require just a general explanation, others do call for deeper direct instruction and modeling. The knowledge and experience your students bring to the task will determine how much instruction is needed. You'll notice that students become more and more independent in tackling the activities as time passes.

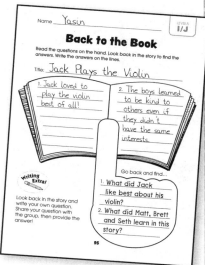

- **Differentiate the activities as needed.** The complexity of the activities varies by level. In the earliest levels, for example, students typically have the option of writing or drawing their responses. As students grow more skilled, pages may ask for responses in key words, sentences, or paragraphs. But don't hesitate to change the directions if they seem beyond what your students can do. For example, if students are not yet writing, let them discuss their responses quietly with a partner. Whenever possible, have an adult present to refocus students as needed. Be sure that students understand how to write a sentence or a paragraph before you ask them to do it alone. Goals should be realistic so that students can be successful.

- **Take time to assess.** Remember that independent activities still require teacher involvement and review; guidance and timely feedback will ultimately result in future independence. After students complete the activities, be sure to allow time to review their work and provide prompt feedback so they can understand what they did well and where they need to improve. Completed pages that show poor or excellent comprehension may trigger a reevaluation of a student's guided reading level. On pages 167–171, you'll find some generic checklists that can help you collect valuable information about student progress.

## Extending the Learning

At the bottom of most of the reproducibles, you will see an extension activity designed to develop students' writing skills. Because students at levels A/B are typically pre-writers or just beginning to write, I have made the extensions at these levels prompts for oral shares (look for the heading "Extra! Extra!"). Students can share their ideas aloud with you or any adult; the adult can help teach, redirect, and focus the students so the skills are learned correctly. The helping adult can also act as a scribe, modeling the writing process.

At the higher levels, the extension activity is called "Writing Extra!" and may call for students to create a list, write a sentence or two, or even write a full paragraph. Sentence-writing practice builds students' paragraph-development skills and improves overall writing abilities. These activities can be completed on regular white lined paper or construction paper, but you'll find a variety of ready-to-copy templates on pages 162–166 that work well for the writing extensions. Keep in mind each student's abilities as you assign the writing extensions; you can certainly have a student draw or orally share a response if the writing task is too challenging for him or her.

You can also extend the activities by inviting students to apply what they have learned in a collaborative task. The Team-Building activities that appear on pages 150–161 allow children to work on group projects in response to the literature they have shared. These activities are not leveled and have been designed for use with a wide range of leveled texts. They make an excellent complement to the leveled independent activities.

Enjoy!

# Leveled Activities

# New Cover

In this activity, students create a new cover for a selected book. To do so, they must distinguish between what is important and what is not important to the story.

### Preparation

Choose a book for students to read or have them choose appropriate books for their reading levels. If you'd like, fill in the title before making copies.

**1.** Have students write the book title if you have not filled it in.

**2.** Have students draw a new cover picture. Remind them that the cover usually gives clues about the story content. If students wish, they can use the page for a rough draft and create the new cover on drawing paper.

### Optional

For the Extra! Extra! activity, have students describe their new cover design and create a new title. Have a discussion to encourage students to support their choices.

# New Cover

Draw a new cover for your book.

Title: _____

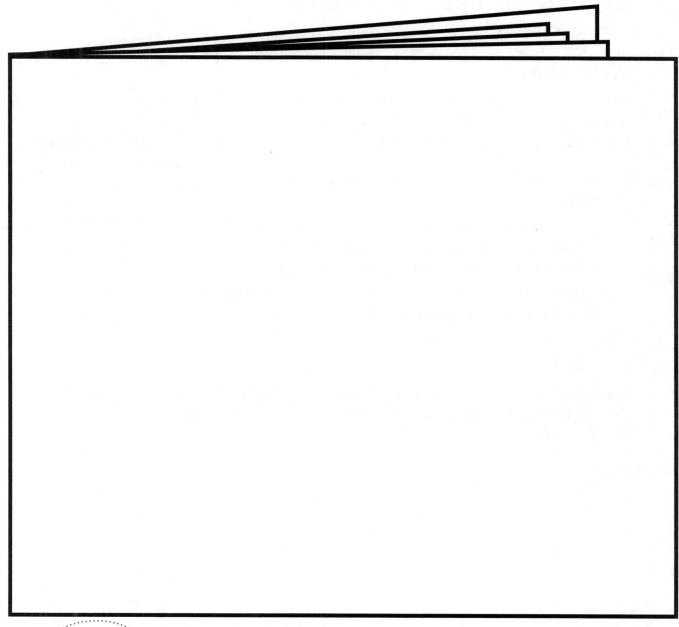

Leveled Reading-Response Activities for Guided Reading © 2013 by Rhonda Graff, Scholastic Teaching Resources

**Extra!
Extra!** Tell an adult about your new cover design and create a new title.

# Say It Again

Here, students engage in a simple retelling of the story. Retelling is a chance for students to process what they have read and demonstrate comprehension.

## Preparation

Choose a book for students to read or have them choose appropriate books for their reading levels. If you'd like, fill in the title before making copies.

1. Have students write the book title if you have not filled it in.

2. In Box 1, instruct students to draw the main characters and/or write the characters' names. Let students know that some books may only have one character.

3. In Boxes 2 and 3, have students draw two important story events. Encourage them to put the events in the correct order.

## Optional

For the Extra! Extra! activity, have the students use the information in all three boxes to retell the story to you or another adult. Check for understanding.

Name _____

# Say It Again

Choose a book. In Box 1, draw the characters and/or write their names. In Boxes 2 and 3, draw and/or write two story events in order.

Title: _____

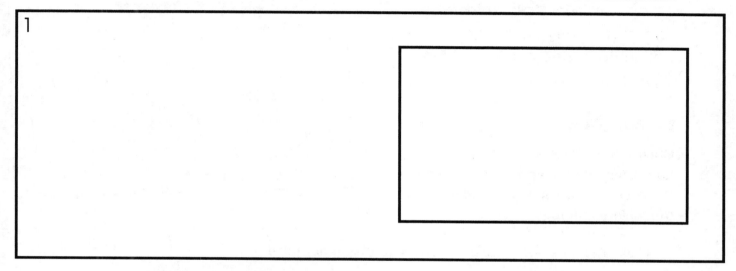

1

2

3

Extra! Extra! Use the boxes to retell the story to an adult.

# My Book Character

In this activity, students think back to remember actions taken by a character in the story. In more advanced texts, children need to understand the characters and their actions to better understand the development of the plot.

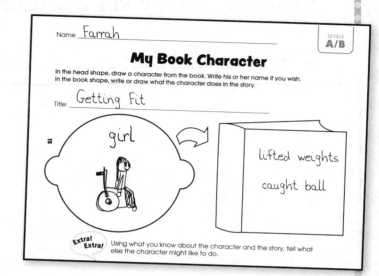

## Preparation

Choose a book for students to read or have them choose appropriate books for their reading levels. If you'd like, fill in the title before making copies.

1. Have students write the book title if you have not filled it in.

2. Have the students look back in the story and choose a character. In the head shape, they can draw the character and/or write the character's name.

3. In the book shape, have students draw or write something the character did in the story. They can provide more than one event if they wish.

## Optional

For the Extra! Extra! activity, have students suggest something else this character might do based on what they already know from the story. Students should think of something that is not in the story.

Name _____

# My Book Character

In the head shape, draw a character from the book. Write his or her name if you wish. In the book shape, write or draw what the character does in the story.

Title: _____

**15**

Extra! Extra!

Using what you know about the character and the story, tell what else the character might like to do.

*Leveled Reading-Response Activities for Guided Reading* © 2013 by Rhonda Graff, Scholastic Teaching Resources

# The Big Idea

This activity encourages students to think about main idea, a crucial component of reading comprehension. They will practice identifying the most important idea in a story.

## Preparation

Choose a book for students to read or have them choose appropriate books for their reading levels.

1. Have students write the book title if you have not filled it in.

2. Explain that the big idea or main idea is what a story is mostly about.

3. Model finding the main idea using another text the students have read. Name or list some details from the book and then think aloud about what these details all have in common (for example, the details are all about fruits we eat). Explain that this is the main idea.

4. Have students think about the details in the story that you or they have selected for this activity. Have them identify what the book is mostly about and draw and/or write it in the light bulb shape. Students need not write a complete sentence.

## Optional

Have students complete the Extra! Extra! activity by describing the story's main idea to a parent, teacher, or other adult.

# The Big Idea

Draw and/or write what your book is mostly about. This is called the main idea.

Title: _____

Extra!
Extra!

Tell an adult about your book's main idea. Share some interesting details.

# Picture Write!

Although pictures don't teach children to read, they do support the text and can even provide information the words do not. This activity encourages students to notice details and gather important information from illustrations in a book.

## Preparation

Choose a book for students to read or have them choose appropriate books for their reading levels. If you'd like, fill in the title before making copies.

**1.** Have students write the book title if you have not already filled it in.

**2.** Remind students that pictures can support or add to a story. Encourage students to look closely at the illustrations in the selected book.

**3.** Have the students write a list of what they see on the lines provided. Remind them that lists do not need complete sentences, only important words.

**4.** Encourage the students to share in small groups. By sharing, students may catch details they otherwise missed.

## Optional

For the Extra! Extra! activity, have students use the words on their lists to tell you or another adult about the story.

Name _____

# Picture Write!

Look at the illustrations in your book. Write a list of things you see.

Title: _____

**I see**

Use the words on your list to tell an adult about the story.

**19**

# Story Snapshot

By making statements about a favorite part of a book, students begin to think about and interact with the text.

## Preparation

Choose a book for students to read or have them choose appropriate books for their reading levels. If you'd like, fill in the title before making copies.

1. Have students write the book title if you have not already filled it in.

2. Have students choose a favorite event from the story and draw it inside the picture box.

3. Encourage students to say aloud to a partner one statement about the chosen event. For example, the statement can give a detail about the event.

## Optional

Have students complete the Extra! Extra! activity by telling you or another adult why they chose this part of the book.

Name _____

# Story Snapshot

Choose a book. Draw your favorite event from the story. Share aloud a statement about your picture.

Title: _____

Extra! Extra!

Tell an adult why you like this part of the book.

Leveled Reading-Response Activities for Guided Reading © 2013 by Rhonda Graff, Scholastic Teaching Resources

# Similar Stories

Comparing and contrasting texts is a key skill in the Common Core State Standards for primary students. This activity will help your students get started.

## Preparation

Choose two books that students have read, or have them choose appropriate books for their reading levels. If you'd like, fill in the titles before making copies.

1. Have students write the two book titles on lines 1 and 2 if you have not already filled them in.

2. Review the organizer on the page. Explain that responses for the first book will go in the box with the 1. Responses for the second book will go in the box with the 2.

3. Have students think of a way the two books are alike. Have them draw and/or write this observation in the boxes. The similarity can be as simple as both main characters being girls or both stories having to do with sports.

## Optional

Have students extend their thinking with the Extra! Extra! activity. Have them describe to a partner one way the two books are different.

Name _____

# Similar Stories

Choose two books. Write and/or draw one way the two books are the same.

Title 1: _____

Title 2: _____

*Leveled Reading-Response Activities for Guided Reading* © 2013 by Rhonda Graff, Scholastic Teaching Resources

Tell a partner about one way the two books are different.

# Make a Prediction

Students can gather information and mix it with their own prior knowledge to make predictions. It is important to have readers start predicting early.

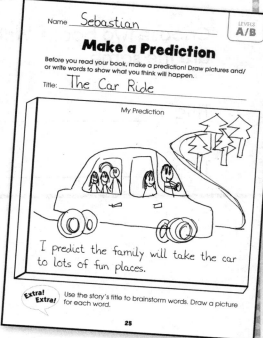

## Preparation

Choose a book for students to read or have them choose appropriate books for their reading levels. It should be one that is completely new to students. If you'd like, fill in the title before making copies.

1. Have students write the book title if you have not already filled it in.

2. Review what a prediction is. Discuss with students what weather forecasters do when they make a prediction (they use observations to guess what the weather will be like tomorrow). Explain that in a book prediction, we use what we know to guess what the book will be about.

3. Have students read the title and look carefully at the cover picture for clues.

4. Have them draw and/or write their predictions for the story in the space provided.

5. Have students discuss in small groups the reasons they made their predictions. Did they use the cover photo or illustration? Did they use the title? Did they make a connection to another book or use their own knowledge of the topic? By sharing, students can see alternate ways to make predictions.

## Optional

The Extra! Extra! activity asks students to brainstorm words that relate to the story's title. Encourage students to do this using a web organizer (see page 163).

# **Make a Prediction**

Before you read your book, make a prediction! Draw pictures and/ or write words to show what you think will happen.

Title: _____

My Prediction

Use the story's title to brainstorm words. Draw a picture for each word.

# Sentence Scramble

In this activity, students cut out and manipulate words to recreate a familiar sentence from the story. This builds fluency and reviews left-to-right directionality and one-to-one word correspondence.

## Preparation

Choose a book that students have read. Before you make copies of the reproducible, choose a sentence from the book and write the words from the sentence in the boxes at the bottom of the page. Scramble them so that they are not in order. Write the ending punctuation mark in one box. (Note: You may choose to use an original sentence instead of one from a book.)

1. Have students cut out the words and punctuation and rearrange them so that the sentence can be read correctly.

2. On the lines, have students glue the words and punctuation in order to correctly form the sentence.

3. Invite students to illustrate the sentence in the box provided.

4. Have students read their sentences aloud to a partner to practice reading with fluency and intonation.

## Optional

You can extend the activity by having students copy the sentence on another piece of paper, using appropriate capitalization, spacing, and punctuation.

# Sentence Scramble

Cut out the words and put them in order. Paste them on the lines. In the box, draw a picture to go with the sentence.

# Word Trace

In texts for A/B readers, you'll find that certain words are repeated with great frequency. This activity is a fantastic way to practice reading, spelling, and writing those high-frequency words.

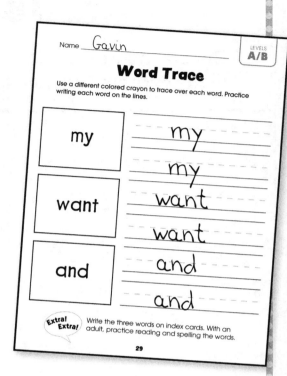

## Preparation

Choose a book that students have read. Before you make copies of the reproducible, select three high-frequency words from the story. Write one word in each box on the left side of the page; print the words as big and as neatly as you can. (Note: You may also include other high-frequency words that you would like to introduce or review.)

1. Be sure your students know how to read the words you have selected. Teach them to say each letter as they trace it with a finger. Have them repeat the word after they finish tracing the letters—for example, *m-e, me*.

2. Have students work independently to trace over each word multiple times with crayon. Encourage them to continue saying the letters softly as they write the word.

3. Then have the students practice writing each high-frequency word on the lines provided.

## Optional

For the Extra! Extra! activity provide large index cards so students can create high-frequency word cards for practice. Students should work with an adult at first to be sure they are practicing correctly.

LEVELS
A/B

# Word Trace

Use a different colored crayon to trace over each word. Practice
writing each word on the lines.

Write the three words on index cards. With an
adult, practice reading and spelling the words.

# Busy Character

It is important for children to be able to understand characters through their actions, thoughts and later on, dialogue. Here, students explore what a character's actions tell readers about that character.

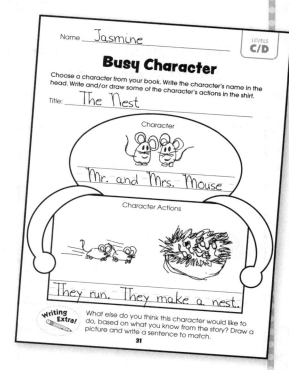

## Preparation

Choose a book for students to read or have them choose appropriate books for their reading levels. If you'd like, fill in the title before making copies.

1. Have students write the book title if you have not already filled it in.

2. Have students choose a character from the story and write the character's name in the head. Have students draw the character in the space provided. Remind students to capitalize the name and to look in the book for the correct spelling.

3. In the shirt portion of the illustration, have students list some of the character's actions in the story. Students can also illustrate the actions in the space provided. Encourage students to focus on actions that are important to the story or especially interesting.

## Optional

For the Writing Extra! activity, have students make inferences about the character. They already know quite a bit about the character's behavior. Have them use what they know to brainstorm something else the character would like to do. For instance, if the story is about the character eating fruit, a student may choose to draw the character eating another healthy snack. Have students write a sentence to match the illustration or share verbally.

# Busy Character

Choose a character from your book. Write the character's name in the head. Write and/or draw some of the character's actions in the shirt.

Title: _____

Character

_____
- - - - - - - - - - - - - - - - - - - -

Character Actions

_____
- - - - - - - - - - - - - - - - - - - -
_____

What else do you think this character would like to do, based on what you know from the story? Draw a picture and write a sentence to match.

*Leveled Reading-Response Activities for Guided Reading © 2013 by Rhonda Graff, Scholastic Teaching Resources*

# Setting the Scene

In this activity, students learn that the setting of a story involves both place and time. They'll also begin thinking about how setting can impact the outcome of a story.

## Preparation

Choose a book for students to read or have them choose appropriate books for their reading levels. Be sure the book has a clear setting. If you'd like, fill in the title before making copies.

1. Have students write the book title if you have not already filled it in.

2. Have students look back in the text to answer the question, *Where does the story take place?* Tell students that they may find clues in the illustrations or in the details of the story (for example, if the characters are on swings, they may be at a park).

3. On the left side of the reproducible, have them write this aspect of the setting. If the setting changes during the story, students can list several or choose one. Have them draw a picture to match.

4. Next, have students answer the question, *When does the story take place?* Explain that this may include the time of day or the time of year. It can also be as simple as "long ago" or "modern times." Have students record this aspect of setting on the right side of the reproducible and draw a picture to match.

## Optional

The Writing Extra! activity invites students to think about the story with an alternative setting. Have them draw the new setting and write or discuss how the new setting would change the story. This will require adult guidance as it is abstract and the children will need to have an adult lead this discussion.

Name _____

# Setting the Scene

Think about the setting of your book. Write your responses to the questions. Then draw pictures to match.

Title: _____

| Where does the story take place? |
| :--- |

| When does the story take place? |
| :--- |

**Writing Extra!**

Can you think of a new setting for the story? Draw the new setting. Tell how it might change the story.

*Leveled Reading-Response Activities for Guided Reading* © 2013 by Rhonda Graff, Scholastic Teaching Resources

# Problem Solved

Most good stories revolve around a problem and end with a satisfying solution. Here, students explore this basic fiction text structure.

## Preparation

Choose a book for students to read or have them choose appropriate books for their reading levels. Be sure the books have a clear problem and solution. If you'd like, fill in the title before making copies.

1. Have students write the book title if you have not already filled it in.

2. Review the concepts of problem and solution using the images on the reproducible: The thirsty flower is drooping (PROBLEM). We pour water on it (SOLUTION).

3. Have students identify the problem in the story and draw or write it in the flowerpot. If they illustrate the problem, be sure they can verbally explain their picture.

4. Have them identify the solution. Have them write or illustrate their responses in the watering can.

## Optional

Use the Writing Extra! activity to further explore problem and solution. Have students illustrate a problem they had and how they solved it. Have them write sentences to match their pictures and share their responses.

Name _____

# Problem Solved

What problem happens in your book? Write or draw it on the flowerpot.
How does the problem get solved? Write or draw it on the watering can.

Title: _____

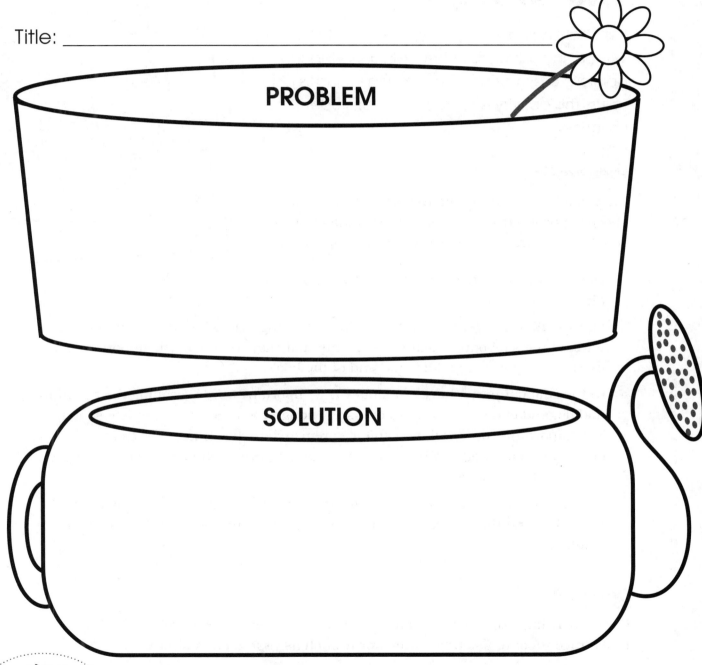

PROBLEM

SOLUTION

**Writing Extra!** Draw a picture showing a problem you had and how you solved it. Write words or sentences to match your picture.

# Sail Through the Story

It is challenging for a young child to retell a story without including his or her opinion. Although opinions are important, a retelling includes just the facts. This activity is a great way for students to practice.

## Preparation

Choose a book for students to read or have them choose appropriate books for their reading levels. If you'd like, fill in the title before making copies.

1. Have students write the book title if you have not already filled it in.

2. Draw students' attention to the labels "Beginning," "Middle," and "End" on the parts of the sailboat. Explain to students that they will recall the important events from the beginning, middle, and end of the book.

3. In the sailboat parts, have students write important words recalling the beginning, middle, and end of the story (there isn't enough room to write complete sentences). The important words will help children remember what is key. For example, instead of writing that a dog and his owner went to the park, a child can list "dog, owner, park" as the key words.

4. Have students use their key words to practice retelling the story to a partner or adult. Remind them to retell the facts and to leave out their own feelings and opinions.

## Optional

For the Writing Extra! activity, have students write sentences to retell the story. Encourage them to use time-order words such as *first*, *then*, and *next*.

# Sail Through the Story

Choose a book. Retell the story in order. Use key words and pictures.

Title: _____

Beginning

Middle

_____
- - - - - - - - - - - - -
_____
- - - - - - - - - - - - -
_____

_____
- - - - - - - - - - - - -
_____
- - - - - - - - - - - - -
_____

End

_____
- - - - - - - - - - - - - - - - - - - - - -
_____

**Writing Extra!**

Use your key words to write sentences about the story events.

# Cause and Effect

Story events are interrelated, often in a cause-and-effect fashion. By recognizing this connection, students can better understand a story.

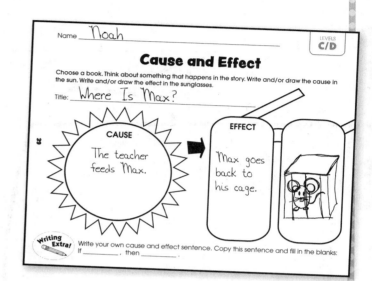

## Preparation

Choose a book for students to read or have them choose appropriate books for their reading levels. If you'd like, fill in the title before making copies. To simplify the activity, you may wish to fill in either a cause or an effect from the story before copying. To make it more challenging, leave both cause and effect blank for students to identify.

1. Have students write the book title if you have not already filled it in.

2. Review with students that in real life and in stories, one thing often causes another to happen. Provide plenty of examples, including the imagery from the page: When it is sunny out (CAUSE), we need to wear sunglasses (EFFECT).

3. If you have already filled in a cause from the story, point it out. Challenge students to identify and then write and draw the corresponding effect in the sunglasses. (If you have filled in an effect, challenge students to write the cause in the sun.)

4. If you'd like students to fill in both parts of the reproducible, have them write and draw any cause and effect from the story.

## Optional

For additional practice, have students complete the Writing Extra! prompt. Be ready to provide causes if students get stuck: "If it is very hot . . . "; "If the boy jumps in the puddle . . . "; and so on. Have students illustrate the sentences. Collect them for a class book!

Name _____

# Cause and Effect

Choose a book. Think about something that happens in the story. Write and/or draw the cause in the sun. Write and/or draw the effect in the sunglasses.

Title: _____

**EFFECT**

**CAUSE**

**Writing Extra!**  Write your own cause and effect sentence. Copy this sentence and fill in the blanks:

If _____, then _____.

# Picture Lists

Although reliance on picture clues cannot replace decoding skills, pictures can help tell a story. By recording and categorizing the items they observe in a busy illustration, students will boost visual literacy and organizational skills.

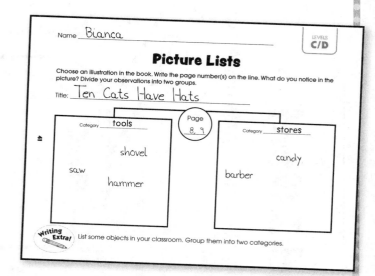

Name Bianca

**Picture Lists**

Choose an illustration in the book. Write the page number(s) on the line. What do you notice in the picture? Divide your observations into two groups.

Title: Ten Cats Have Hats

Category __tools__          Page 8, 9          Category __stores__

shovel                                              candy

saw                                     barber

hammer

**Writing Extra!** List some objects in your classroom. Group them into two categories.

## Preparation

Choose a book for students to read or have them choose appropriate books for their reading levels. If you'd like, fill in the title before making copies. You may also wish to preselect the illustration students will use for the activity and record it before copying. If your students are new to this activity, it's a good idea to preselect and label the categories for their observations as well. Examples of categories may include characters, setting, toys, animals, and foods.

1. Have students write the book title if you have not already filled it in.

2. Have students browse the book and choose an illustration if you have not preselected one. Instruct them to record the page number(s) on the line provided.

3. If you have preselected categories for the students to work with, have students study the illustration and look for items that fall into those categories. Instruct the students to write or draw responses under the correct headings on the handout.

4. If students are choosing their own categories, have them record the category titles on the tops of the lists before listing the items that fall into those categories.

## Optional

Extend the activity by having students classify objects. They can sort actual objects or they can put objects into categories—for example, Things We Use for Art and Fall Things.

Name _____

# Picture Lists

Choose an illustration in the book. Write the page number(s) on the line. What do you notice in the picture? Divide your observations into two groups.

Title: _____

Category _____

Category _____

Page _____

**Writing Extra!**

List some objects in your classroom. Group them into two categories.

**41**

# Book Detective

Have students hunt for ways that two fictional characters are alike—and boost comprehension in the process!

## Preparation

For this activity, students compare two characters from the same book or from different books. Choose one or two books for students to read, according to your preference. If you'd like, preselect the characters students will compare and record the names before copying.

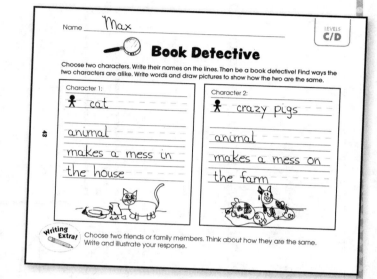

1. Have students select two characters to compare and write their names on the lines, if you have not already done so.

2. Discuss ways that people (or characters) can be alike: They may share physical features, talents, interests, or personality characteristics. They may have similar experiences or face similar problems.

3. Have children go back into the book(s) and identify similarities between the two characters. It is good practice for them to look back, reread, review, and confirm what took place in the story rather than rely on memory. Some similarities may be found in the pictures. Students should record the similarities in the character columns (using either key words or sentences).

4. Provide support and prompts as needed if students struggle.

5. Have students illustrate their writing.

## Optional

Use the Writing Extra! activity to provide additional practice making comparisons.

Name _____

# Book Detective

Choose two characters. Write their names on the lines. Then be a book detective! Find ways the two characters are alike. Write words and draw pictures to show how the two are the same.

Character 1:

👤 _____

| | |
| | |
| | |
| | |

Character 2:

👤 _____

| | |
| | |
| | |
| | |

**Writing Extra!**

Choose two friends or family members. Think about how they are the same. Write and illustrate your response.

# What's Cooking?

Multiple meaning words (*bat, set, roll,* etc.) are found in even the earliest reading materials. Introducing these words early on will help students improve overall comprehension.

## Preparation

Before copying the reproducible, you'll need to preselect a word with multiple meanings. It can be a word from a book that students have just read or will read soon, or it can be chosen from the list on page 174. Write the word on the page before reproducing.

1. Have students read the word. Discuss as a class or have students discuss in pairs two meanings for the word.

2. Help students write a very brief definition in the top pot. Then have students illustrate that word in the same pot.

3. Have students write and illustrate the second meaning of the word in the second pot.

4. You may occasionally come across a word that has more than two meanings. If students wish, they can write and illustrate additional meanings on the back of the page.

## Optional

Vocabulary exposure enhances comprehension. Have students use the multiple-meaning word from this activity in two original sentences, one for each meaning.

Name _____

# What's Cooking?

Some words have more than one meaning. Look at the word on the lines. In the first pot, write and draw one meaning. In second pot, write and draw another meaning for the same word.

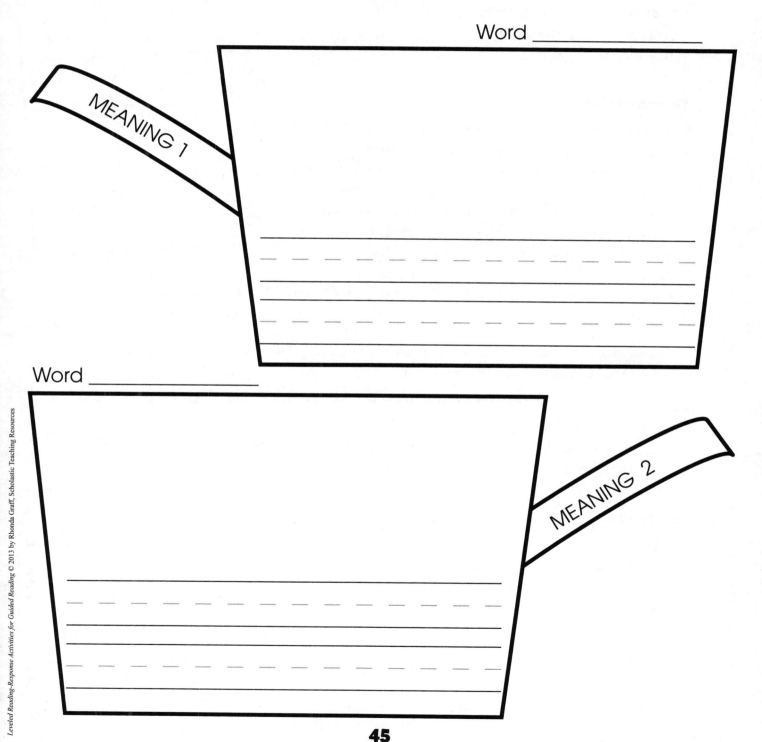

Word _____

MEANING 1

Word _____

MEANING 2

# Bag of Words

This flexible reproducible can be used to review rhyming words, synonyms, contractions, compound words, vowel pairs, digraphs, nouns, or any other focus skill.

## Preparation

Before copying, decide which skill you'd like students to practice. For example, you might have students look for words that rhyme with a key word from the story, nouns from the story, or words from the story that use the digraph *ch*. The possibilities are endless. To provide direction, write the focus skill on the bag's tag. You should also preselect words from the book and write them in the Word Bank. Make sure that not all of the words in the Bank fit the criterion written on the tag. Words do not necessarily need to appear in the book to be used for this activity.

1. Have students read the instruction on the bag's tag. Make sure they understand the kinds of words they are looking for.

2. Have students use the Word Bank to choose words that fit the criterion. Have them write the appropriate words on the lines in the bag.

3. If you'd like, have students brainstorm additional words that fit the criterion and use them to create a word chart or booklet.

## Optional

For the Writing Extra! activity, have students write sentences (both statements and questions) using some of the words from the bag.

LEVELS
C/D

# Bag of Words

Read the tag on the bag. Decide which words from the Word Bank belong in the bag. Write them on the lines.

**Word Bank**

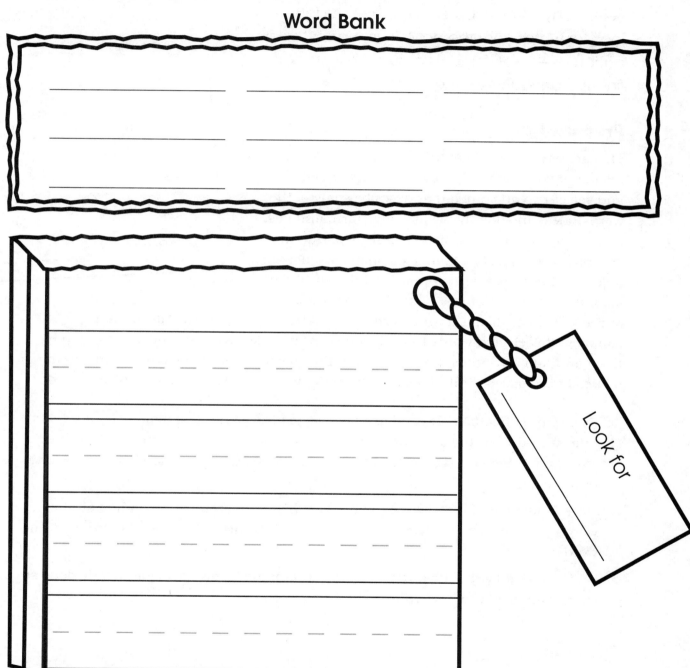

Look for

**Writing Extra!**

Write sentences using some of the words from your bag. Include some statements and some questions.

# Word Sort

Select any two attributes and have students look for words from the book that match those attributes—or let students group the words and find the attributes on their own.

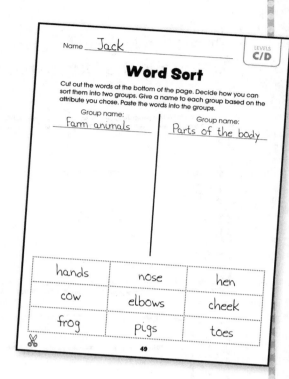

## Preparation

This activity can be done with varying degrees of teacher involvement. If you wish, review a book and select two attributes that describe some of the words. Ideas include themes such as farm animals, food, character traits, or modes of transportation. Attributes can also be skill-based such as synonyms, adjectives, or words with specific blends. Write the attributes in the columns, then fill in the boxes at the bottom of the page with words that match the attributes. Alternatively, simply write selected words from the story in the boxes so that students can group them and find attributes. For example, if the story is about a farm, you can list animal names in the boxes. Children can sort them by name, by number of legs, and so on.

1. Review the directions. If you have preselected the attributes, make sure students understand what the attributes mean. If students are finding attributes on their own, guide them to understand that they are looking for characteristics the words have in common.

2. Have students cut out the boxes and sort them into groups. Depending on the words you have chosen, you might note that students do not need to use all of the words.

3. Have students write the attributes on the columns if you have not already done so. Have them paste each word into the correct column.

## Optional

If students develop their own attributes, have them explain how they decided on the attributes. If students sorted words into preselected groups, have them try to add more words to each group.

# Word Sort

Cut out the words at the bottom of the page. Decide how you can sort them into two groups. Give a name to each group based on the attribute you chose. Paste the words into the groups.

Group name: _____        Group name: _____

Leveled Reading-Response Activities for Guided Reading © 2013 by Rhonda Graff, Scholastic Teaching Resources

# People and Places

Review the basic story elements of characters and setting as students engage with a favorite work of fiction.

## Preparation

Choose a book for students to read or have them choose appropriate books for their reading levels. If you'd like, fill in the title before making copies.

1. Have students write the book title if you have not already filled it in.

2. Have students identify two main characters and write the names in the windows. If the book has only one character, students can leave one window blank. If the character does not have a name, have children write "boy" or "dog" to identify the character as best they can. Have students add drawings of the characters.

3. Review the definition of setting and make sure that students know that setting involves both where and when the story takes place. Students may need help thinking about the time element; point out that it can be very general (modern times) or very specific (Thanksgiving morning), depending on the book.

4. Have students describe and draw the setting on the first floor of the house.

## Optional

Use the Writing Extra! activity to have students generate lists of words that describe each main character and the setting.

# People and Places

Choose a book. In each window, write the name of a character from the story. At the bottom of the house, write and draw the setting. The setting is where and when the story takes place.

Title: _____

Character

Character

Setting

Make a list of words to describe each character. Make a third list of words to describe the setting.

# Wheel Away the Problem

Identifying problem and solution is critical to comprehension of most fiction texts. This activity provides a fun way to practice.

## Preparation

Choose a book for students to read or have them choose appropriate books for their reading levels. If you'd like, fill in the title before making copies.

1. Have students write the book title if you have not already filled it in.

2. Review the concepts of problem and solution using examples from everyday life. The imagery on the page offers one example: If we have rocks in the yard (PROBLEM), we can wheel them away (SOLUTION).

3. In the rocks atop the wheelbarrow, have students identify the main problem(s) in the story. Since space is limited, students may choose to use key words instead of complete sentences.

4. On the wheelbarrow, have students write the solution to the problem. Encourage children to go back into the story if they cannot remember the events clearly.

## Optional

Provide additional practice with problem and solution with the Writing Extra! activity Have students write about a problem they had at school or at home and describe how they overcame it.

Name _____

# Wheel Away the Problem

Think of the main problem in the story. Write it in the rocks. Recall how the problem got solved. Write it in the wheelbarrow.

Title: _____

Problem:
_____
_____
_____
_____

Solution:
_____
_____
_____
_____
_____

**Writing Extra!**

Write about a problem you had. Explain how you solved it. Draw a picture to match.

# Cool Characters

This bookmark will help students better understand the characters they meet in stories. Make two copies so that students can compare and contrast two characters!

## Preparation

Choose a book for students to read or have them choose appropriate books for their reading levels. If you'd like, fill in the character name and book title before making copies. Note: If you'd like students to compare two characters, make double copies of the reproducible and choose two characters from the same book or different books.

1. Have students write the character name and book title if you have not already done so.

2. Have students go back into the story and answer the questions *What does the character do?* and *How does the character feel?* Space is limited, so students can use key words and phrases instead of complete sentences. If you wish, make the list of character-trait words on page 174 available to students as they work.

3. If you'd like students to compare characters, distribute another copy of the reproducible and repeat step 2. Have students discuss as a class or in pairs how the two characters are alike or different.

4. Encourage students to cut out the bookmark(s) and illustrate the character(s) on the back.

## Optional

Make copies of the bookmark available for students to use—and fill in—each time they read a new fiction book. Use tagboard for sturdier construction and have students add string or lace to the top.

Name _____

# Cool Characters

Choose a character from your book. In the bookmark, write the character's name and the book title. Then, write what the character does and how he or she feels. Cut out the bookmark and draw the character on the back.

Character
_____
_____

Title
_____
_____
_____

What does the character do?
_____
_____
_____
_____

How does the character feel?
_____
_____
_____
_____

# Pop the Question!

In this versatile activity, prompt students to revisit and recall important details from the story.

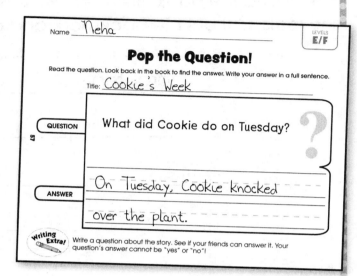

## Preparation

Choose a book for students to read or have them choose appropriate books for their reading levels. If you'd like, fill in the title before making copies. Before copying, you will also need to provide a question for students to answer about the story. In the beginning, focus on questions that are answered directly in the text. Later, as students become more proficient, include questions that call on students to make inferences and think beyond the text.

1. Have students write the book title if you have not already done so.

2. Have students read the question about the story. If necessary, offer a hint (such as a page number or scene description) to help students find the answers.

3. Have students write the answer to the question on the lines in the bottom of the ice pop.

## Optional

The Writing Extra! activity prompts students to write a question about the story to ask a friend. Remind students to go beyond yes/no questions. Encourage them to share their question with a partner, and ask partners to respond in complete sentences. Have an adult present to guide and monitor the discussion and to check for accuracy.

Name _____

# Pop the Question!

Read the question. Look back in the book to find the answer. Write your answer in a full sentence.

Title: _____

**QUESTION**

**ANSWER**

**Writing Extra!** Write a question about the story. See if your friends can answer it. Your question's answer cannot be "yes" or "no"!

# Put It in Order

Reviewing the sequence of key events in a story is an important step in retelling.

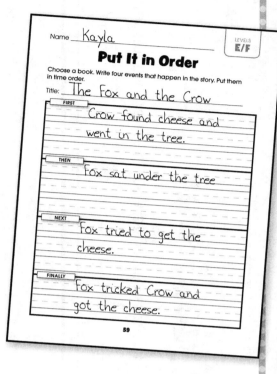

## Preparation

Choose a book for students to read or have them choose appropriate books for their reading levels. If you'd like, fill in the title before making copies.

1. Have students write the book title if you have not already done so.

2. Point out the temporal words (*first, then, next,* and *finally*) at the top of the text blocks. Guide students to understand that words like these are used to help organize events in sequential order.

3. Discuss what makes an event important to the story. Guide students to understand that the most important events often show a problem starting, growing, and getting solved.

4. Have students identify four important events from the story in chronological order. Have them write each event in a block. Encourage students to illustrate the four events on the back of the paper.

## Optional

For the Writing Extra! activity, have students brainstorm additional words that signal time order. A web organizer (page 163) is perfect for this exercise.

Name _____

# Put It in Order

Choose a book. Write four events that happen in the story. Put them in time order.

Title: _____

**FIRST**

**THEN**

**NEXT**

**FINALLY**

# Story Message

Because the message of a story is usually implied instead of stated, identifying it can be challenging for students. Here, students will learn to use events from the story to infer the author's intended message.

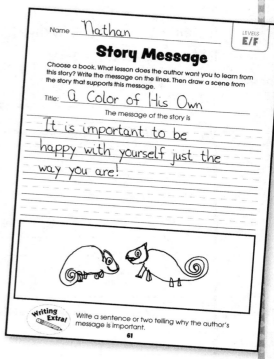

## Preparation

Choose a book for students to read or have them choose appropriate books for their reading levels. If you'd like, fill in the title before making copies.

1. Have students write the book title if you have not already done so.

2. Explain that the message of a story is what the author wants readers to remember. It is often a lesson that the main character learns. Offer examples: A character is afraid he won't have fun camping, but when he goes camping he enjoys his trip after all. The story message is to try new things because you may enjoy them!

3. Have students think about the story they have read and ask themselves: What happened to the character? Did the character learn an important lesson? What's the message the author wanted to share with readers? Finding the message may take a good bit of modeling and instruction at first, but with practice, students will soon be doing it independently.

4. Have students record the message on the lines and draw a scene from the story that supports the message.

## Optional

Have students share their own opinions about the author's message with the Writing Extra! prompt.

# Story Message

Choose a book. What lesson does the author want you to learn from this story? Write the message on the lines. Then draw a scene from the story that supports this message.

Title: _____

The message of the story is
_____

_____

_____

_____

_____

_____

_____

_____

**Writing Extra!**

Write a sentence or two telling why the author's message is important.

# Picture Sort

Though nothing can replace solid decoding, good readers often extract additional information from visuals. In this activity, students will list and organize their observations of a selected illustration.

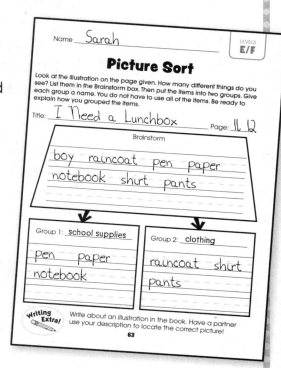

## Preparation

Choose a book for students to read or have them choose appropriate books for their reading levels. Before making copies, fill in the title and identify the page number(s) of the illustration you want the students to respond to. (If there is no page number, have students use a sticky note or bookmark to identify the page in their books.)

1. After reading, have students study the selected illustration. Ask them to list everything they notice in the Brainstorm box.

2. Instruct students to categorize the words into two groups. Be sure students can describe the characteristics they used to form each group. Examples of group pairs might be people and animals, things outside and things inside, and so on. Emphasize that students need not use all of the items they put in the Brainstorm box.

3. Invite students to share how they grouped the items. Be sure that students understand that there is no one "right" answer.

4. Discuss how the illustration helps tell the story. Ask: *What information does the illustration give that the text does not?*

## Optional

For the Writing Extra! activity, ask students to describe another illustration from the story in great detail (either orally or in writing). Have partners try locate the illustrations based on the description.

Name _____

# Picture Sort

Look at the illustration on the page given. How many different things do you see? List them in the Brainstorm box. Then put the items into two groups. Give each group a name. You do not have to use all of the items. Be ready to explain how you grouped the items.

Title: _____ Page: _____

```
Brainstorm
_____
- - - - - - - - - - - - - - - - - - - - - - - -
_____
- - - - - - - - - - - - - - - - - - - - - - - -
_____
- - - - - - - - - - - - - - - - - - - - - - - -
_____
```

Group 1: _____

Group 2: _____

Write about an illustration in the book. Have a partner use your description to locate the correct picture!

**63**

# Fact and Opinion

Distinguishing between facts and opinions is an essential literacy skill. Here, students practice writing facts and opinions about fictional characters.

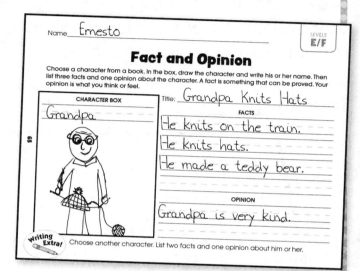

## Preparation

Choose a book for students to read or have them choose appropriate books for their reading levels. If you'd like, fill in the title before making copies.

1. Have students write the book title if you have not already done so.

2. Have students choose a character from the story and write the character's name in the character box. Students should also draw the character in the space provided.

3. Review the differences between facts and opinions. Explain that a fact is a statement that can be proved true. An opinion is a statement that shows what someone thinks or feels. Provide some examples of each.

4. Have students list three facts about the character. They can look back in the story if they need reminders.

5. Invite students to form an opinion about the selected character. Have them write their opinion on the last line.

## Optional

Use the Writing Extra! activity to have students list facts and opinions about a different character. It may be a character from the same story or a different story.

Name _____

# Fact and Opinion

Choose a character from a book. In the box, draw the character and write his or her name. Then list three facts and one opinion about the character. A fact is something that can be proved. Your opinion is what you think or feel.

**CHARACTER BOX**

Title: _____

**FACTS**

**OPINION**

**Writing Extra!** Choose another character. List two facts and one opinion about him or her.

*Leveled Reading-Response Activities for Guided Reading* © 2013 by Rhonda Graff, Scholastic Teaching Resources

# Unlock Word Meaning

Students will encounter multiple-meaning words in most of the books they read. Use this activity to explore such words and improve comprehension.

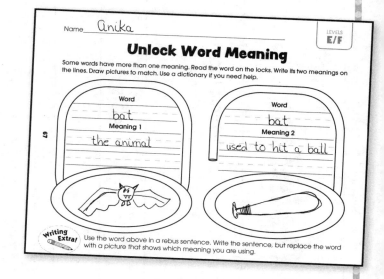

## Preparation

Choose a word with multiple meanings from a book that students have read or will read. Alternatively, select a word from the list on page 174. Before making copies, write the chosen word in the center of each padlock.

1. Direct students' attention to the target word. Explain that it appears twice because it has two meanings.

2. Offer a different multiple-meaning word as an example, giving a simple definition for each meaning. Example: *A set can be a collection or kit, like a chemistry set. Set can also mean to put things in a specific place, like when we set the table.*

3. Have students do the same for the word that appears on the page. Have them write and illustrate one meaning on each padlock. Students should use their own words if possible, but can check a children's dictionary if they need help.

## Optional

Students will have fun with this Writing Extra! activity. Have students use the selected word in a rebus sentence. Have students write a sentence but replace the multiple meaning word with an illustration that shows which meaning is intended. You may want to share some rebuses with students before they give this a try.

Name _____

# Unlock Word Meaning

Some words have more than one meaning. Read the word on the locks. Write its two meanings on the lines. Draw pictures to match. Use a dictionary if you need help.

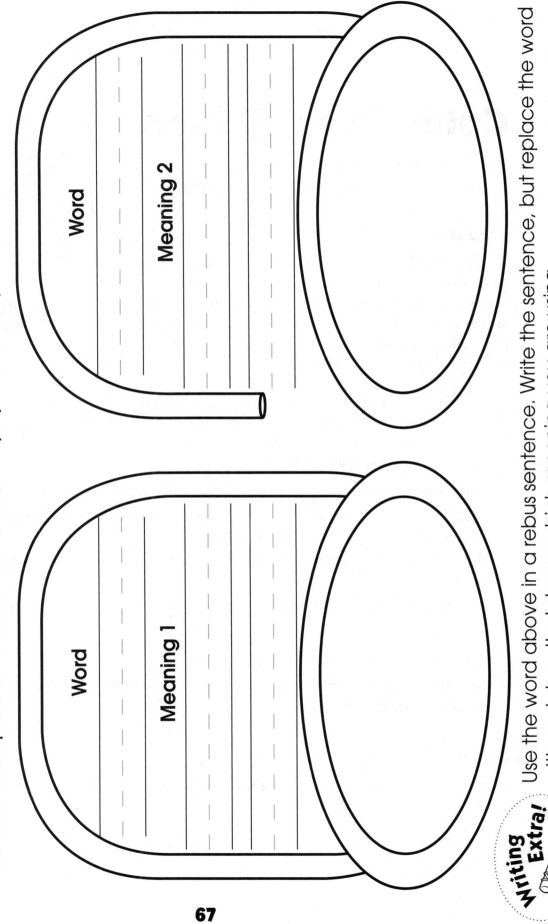

Word

Meaning 1

Word

Meaning 2

**Writing Extra!** Use the word above in a rebus sentence. Write the sentence, but replace the word with a picture that shows which meaning you are using.

*Leveled Reading-Response Activities for Guided Reading © 2013 by Rhonda Graff, Scholastic Teaching Resources*

# Catch Some Fiction

In this activity, students use stories they have read to explore additional characteristics of fiction.

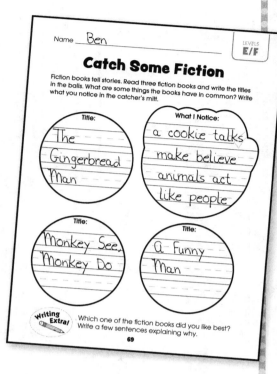

## Preparation

Consider pairing or grouping students for this activity. Assemble a collection of level-appropriate fiction books that students have already read or that they can read for the activity. Try to include various genres such as fairy tales, realistic fiction, fantasy, and fables. Each pair or group will need three fiction texts.

1. Review the directions with students. Explain that the books in the pile are all fiction, or made-up stories. Each pair or group will look at three books and describe what they notice.

2. Have students read or review three books and list the titles on the baseballs.

3. On the catcher's mitt, have pairs or groups record some of the things the books have in common. Circulate through the room to help students note characteristics, draw conclusions, and record information. For example, students may notice the following:

   • Fiction books have characters and a setting.

   • Fiction books have conflicts and resolutions.

   • Fiction books may have talking animals.

4. As a class, discuss the characteristics that students found. Create a master list to display in the classroom.

## Optional

Have students complete the Writing Extra! activity by telling which of the three fiction books they like best and why.

Name _____

# Catch Some Fiction

Fiction books tell stories. Read three fiction books and write the titles in the balls. What are some things the books have in common? Write what you notice in the catcher's mitt.

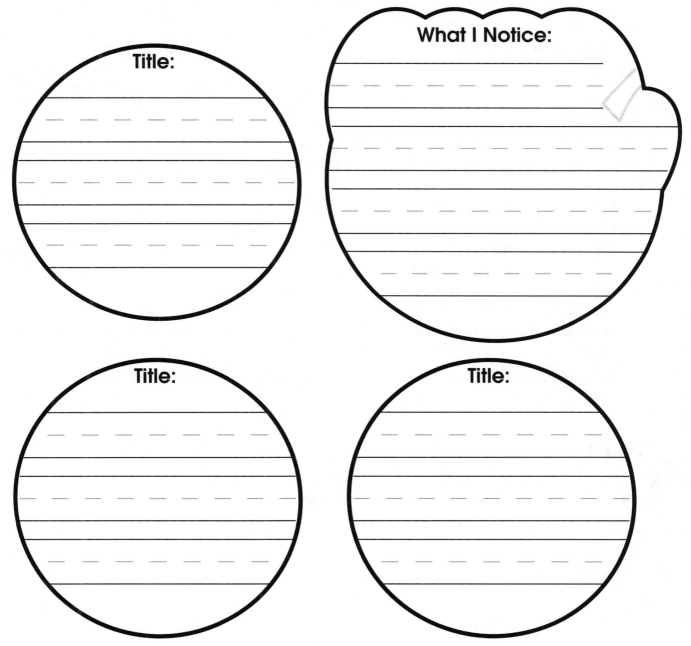

**Title:**

**What I Notice:**

**Title:**

**Title:**

Which one of the fiction books did you like best? Write a few sentences explaining why.

# Super Setting

Setting is an important story element, often dictating the problems characters face and the resources they have to solve those problems. In this activity, students explore the role setting plays in a story.

## Preparation

Choose a book for students to read or have them choose appropriate books for their reading levels.

1. Have students write the book title on the line provided.

2. Have students think about the setting of the story. Remind them that setting includes both place (where the story takes place) and time (when it takes place). A story can have more than one setting, but encourage students to think of the one where most of the important action takes place. Have students draw the setting in the house shape.

3. On the lines provided, have students describe the setting and explain why the setting is important to the story.

## Optional

For the Writing Extra! activity, have students suggest another setting for the same story. Ask them to describe how the new setting might change the story.

# Super Setting

Choose a book. Draw the setting. Then tell why the setting is important to the story.

Title: _____

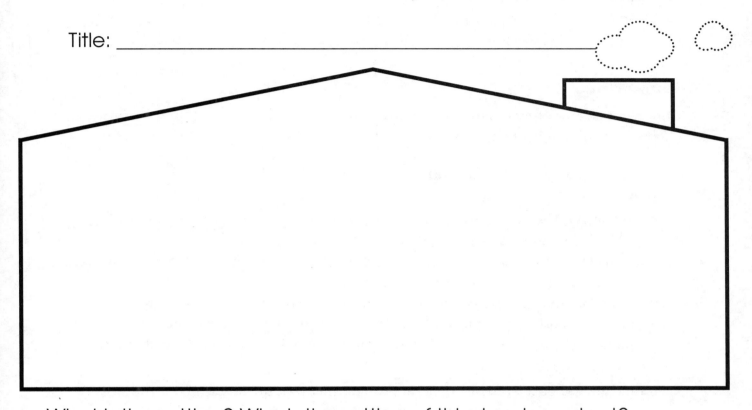

What is the setting? Why is the setting of this story important?

_____
- - - - - - - - - - - - - - - - - - - - - - - - -
_____
_____
_____
- - - - - - - - - - - - - - - - - - - - - - - - -
_____

Can you think of another setting for the story? Describe the new setting and tell how it might change the story.

Leveled Reading-Response Activities for Guided Reading © 2013 by Rhonda Graff, Scholastic Teaching Resources

# Five W's and How

Having students answer the journalistic five W's and How is an excellent way to focus on important details and introduce summarizing skills.

## Preparation

Choose a book for students to read or have them choose appropriate books for their reading levels.

1. Have students write the book title on the line provided.

2. On the chart, have students write key words or sentences to answer: WHO is it about?, WHAT happens? WHERE does it happen? WHEN does it happen? WHY does it happen? and HOW does it end? (Note that the "why" and "how" questions may be posed differently for different stories; you may change the exact wording to suit your needs. For example, instead of "HOW does it end?" you might ask, "HOW does the character feel?")

3. If time allows, have students generate two of their own questions about the story using any of the six question words. Have them write their questions on the back of the page and answer in complete sentences.

## Optional

Have students answer the five W's and How as they complete the Writing Extra! activity about a special day.

---

Name __Julia__

LEVELS
G/H

### Five W's and How

Choose a book. Answer the six questions about the story using key words.

Title: __Popcorn Fun__

| | |
|---|---|
| WHO is it about? | Katie and Joe |
| WHAT happens? | make popcorn |
| WHERE does it happen? | in their house |
| WHEN does it happen? | On a rainy day |
| WHY? | It is yummy and fun. |
| HOW? | They ate all of it ! |

**Writing Extra!** Think about a special day you had. Answer who, what, where, when, why, and how about your day. Illustrate your response.

73

# Five W's and How

Choose a book. Answer the six questions about the story using key words.

Title: _____

| | |
|---|---|
| WHO is it about? | |
| WHAT happens? | |
| WHERE does it happen? | |
| WHEN does it happen? | |
| WHY? | |
| HOW? | |

**Writing Extra!**

Think about a special day you had. Answer *who, what, where, when, why,* and *how* about your day. Illustrate your response.

*Leveled Reading-Response Activities for Guided Reading* © 2013 by Rhonda Graff, Scholastic Teaching Resources

# Story Parts

All three of the main story components (characters, setting, and plot events) come together in this fun organizer.

## Preparation

Choose a book for students to read or have them choose appropriate books for their reading levels.

1. Have students write the book title on the line provided.

2. Remind students that there are many parts to a story including characters, setting, problem, and solution. The plot is the series of events that happen in a story.

3. Have students identify the main character(s) from the story in the face shape.

4. Have students identify the setting in the house shape.

5. Have students choose three key events from the story. Instruct them to write and illustrate the events in order in the three event boxes provided. Point out the sequence words that appear on the boxes: *first, next, finally.*

6. Have children retell the story orally using the information on their handouts.

## Optional

For extra practice retelling events in order, have students complete the Writing Extra! activity. Remind students to use sequencing words as they describe in order key events from their day.

Name Dante

LEVELS G/H

### Story Parts

Name your book's characters and setting. Then write and draw three events from the story. Keep the events in order.

Title: Mr. McCready's Cleaning Day

**Characters**
Mr. McCready
mouse cat
dog

**Setting**
Mr. McCready's house

**First**
Mr. M lost glasses

**Next**
vacuumed mouse, cat, and dog

**Finally**
vacuum exploded had to clean again

**Writing Extra!** List three or four events from your day in order.

75

# Story Parts

Name your book's characters and setting. Then write and draw three events from the story. Keep the events in order.

Title: _____

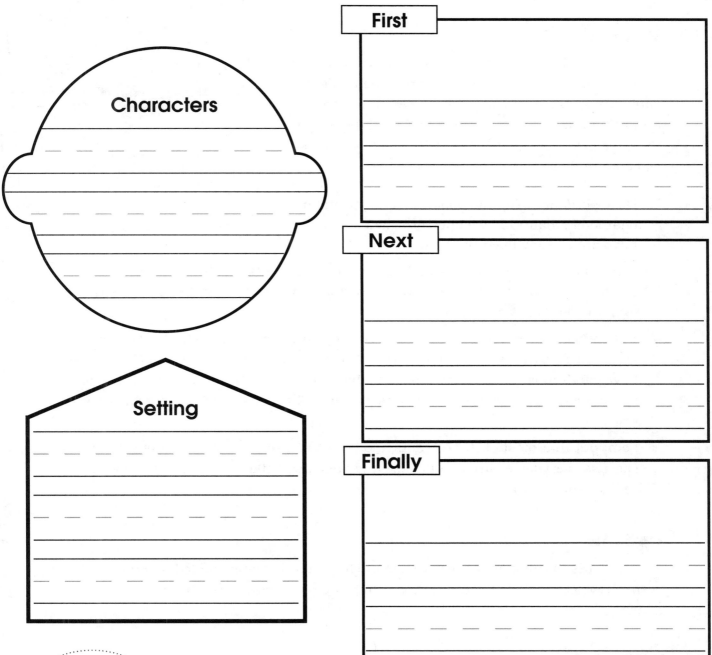

**Characters**

**Setting**

**First**

**Next**

**Finally**

**Writing Extra!** List three or four events from your day in order.

# Character Reaction

Students explore how a character responds to a major story event.

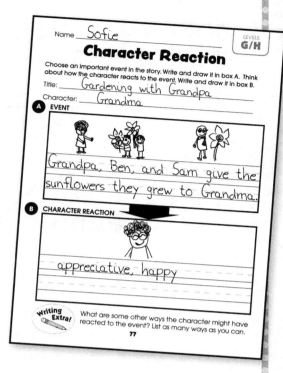

## Preparation

Choose a book for students to read or have them choose appropriate books for their reading levels. If you'd like, you can choose a character and a story event that affects that character and record these on the page before making copies. Otherwise, students will choose these on their own.

1. Have students write the book title and the main character's name on the lines provided if you have not already filled them in.

2. If you have not preselected a story event, have students identify a major event in the story that impacts the character. Have students write and illustrate the event in Box A.

3. Encourage students to think about how the character reacts to that event. Ask: *Does the character's behavior change? Do you know how he or she feels?* In Box B, have children write and draw how the character responds to the event. If you wish, make the list of character trait words on page 174 available to students as they work.

4. Point out that most of these events and reactions are examples of cause and effect. Discuss everyday examples of cause and effect, so children begin to see how these relationships work.

## Optional

Ask students to think about how the character might have responded differently to the event. Have students list some of those alternate reactions as part of the Writing Extra! activity.

Name _____

# Character Reaction

Choose an important event in the story. Write and draw it in box A. Think about how the character reacts to the event. Write and draw it in box B.

Title: _____

Character: _____

**A** **EVENT**

**B** **CHARACTER REACTION**

What are some other ways the character might have reacted to the event? List as many ways as you can.

Leveled Reading-Response Activities for Guided Reading © 2013 by Rhonda Graff, Scholastic Teaching Resources

# In the Details

Recognizing details that relate to a topic from the story helps students develop better comprehension. Learning how to include important details can help students become stronger writers.

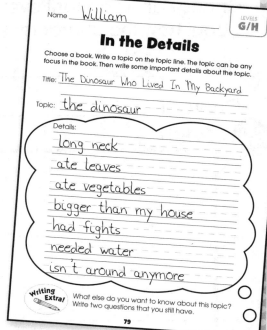

## Preparation

Choose a book for students to read or have them choose appropriate books for their reading levels. If you'd like, choose a topic from the book before making copies; then write it on the line provided. The focus topic may be a character, the setting, the problem, the solution, or another story event. It may also be a theme from the story, such as friendship. If you'd prefer, you can leave it blank and have students choose their own topic to focus on.

1. Have students write the book title on the line provided.

2. Direct students' attention to the topic you have selected, or have them choose an appropriate topic from the book. Give suggestions if needed.

3. Have students note details about the topic in the thought balloon. For example, if the topic is a character, they might include some of the character's actions, his or her appearance, and some character traits he or she possesses.

4. Encourage students to review their details or to work with an adult to make sure all of the details they listed fit the topic.

## Optional

For the Writing Extra! activity, encourage students to record questions they still have about the topic .

# In the Details

Choose a book. Write a topic on the topic line. The topic can be any focus in the book. Then write some important details about the topic.

Title: _____

_____

Topic: _____

Details: _____

**Writing Extra!**

What else do you want to know about this topic? Write two questions that you still have.

# Comparing Characters

Students use a Venn diagram to explore how two characters are alike and different.

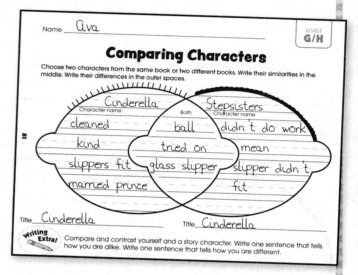

## Preparation

Students may compare characters from the same book or from different books. Choose books for the group according to your preference, or have students choose their own.

1. Have students write the book title(s) on the lines provided.

2. Have students write the characters' names on the lines provided.

3. Model the use of a Venn diagram if students are unfamiliar with this type of organizer. You can compare apples and oranges or soccer and basketball. Space is limited in a Venn diagram, so model using words and phrases instead of complete sentences.

4. Have students begin by brainstorming qualities or experiences the two characters share. Have them write these in the center area where the two faces overlap. If you wish, make the list of character-trait words on page 174 available to students as they work.

5. Have students think of traits or experiences that are unique to one or the other of the characters. They should record each one in the appropriate face shape on the right or left.

## Optional

Extend the learning by having students compare and contrast themselves with a story character. Instead of using a Venn diagram, students write in complete sentences. Encourage students to use transition words such as: *on the other hand*, *meanwhile*, or *similarly*.

Name _____

# Comparing Characters

Choose two characters from the same book or two different books. Write their similarities in the middle. Write their differences in the outer spaces.

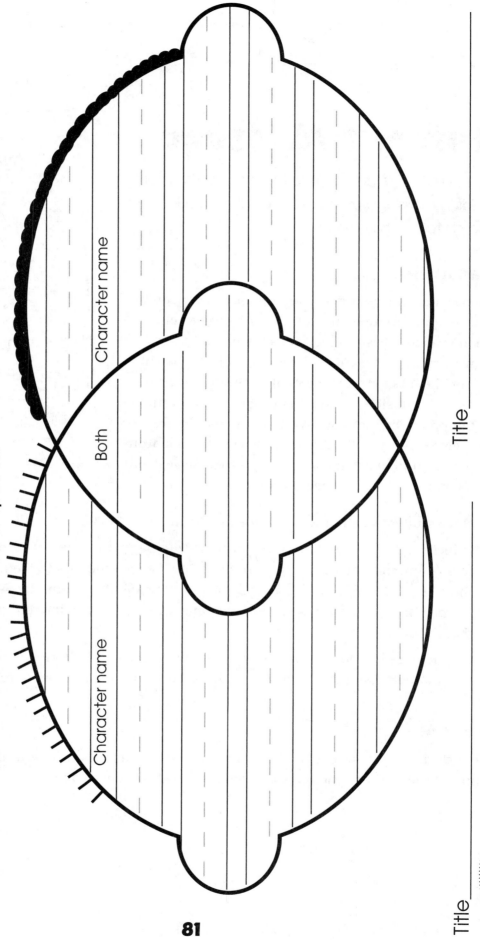

Character name

Both

Character name

Title _____

Title _____

**Writing Extra!** Compare and contrast yourself and a story character. Write one sentence that tells how you are alike. Write one sentence that tells how you are different.

# Author's Message

In this activity, students explore how an author sends a message or lesson through specific events and details in a story.

## Preparation

Choose a book for students to read or have them choose appropriate books for their reading levels. When students first tackle this activity, you may want to identify the author's message on the pencil can for them before making copies. Students will then be responsible for looking for details or events that support the message. As students gain more experience they will be able to draw conclusions from the details and arrive at the message themselves; you can then leave the message lines blank.

1. Have students write the book title on the line provided.

2. Direct students' attention to the author's message you have recorded, if you did this before making copies. Alternatively, challenge students to identify what they think is the important message in the story. Scaffold students by asking: *What lesson does the character learn? What important idea does the author want you to think about?*

3. On the paper outline, have the students write some details or events from the story that support the author's message. Ask: *How does the author share this message?*

## Optional

The Writing Extra! activity invites students to locate an illustration in the book that supports the author's message and write several sentences about the picture.

# Author's Message

Choose a book. What big message does the author share in the story? Write it on the pencil can. What details from the story support this message? Write them on the paper.

Title: _____

Author's message
or lesson

Supporting Details

**Writing Extra!**

Choose an illustration from the story that supports the author's message. Write three sentences describing the illustration.

# Shades of Meaning

This vocabulary lesson helps students understand words with shades of meaning, a skill spotlighted in the Common Core State Standards. Until students are proficient with this skill, this activity may require more adult guidance than most of the other activities in this book.

## Preparation

Choose a word that is closely related in meaning to several other words but whose meaning varies slightly. Examples of such words include *march, walk, strut, jog, run, stride, sprint; cool, chilly, cold, freezing.* You may choose a word from a book that students have read or select one from the list on page 174. Write the word in the framed box before making copies.

1. Give examples of words with shades of meaning. For instance, point out to students that if we want to tell someone something, we can whisper, talk, yell, or even scream. Guide students to understand that these words have related meanings but vary in strength or intensity.

2. Have students read the word in the box and discuss its meaning.

3. On the lines below the box, have students write other words whose definitions are similar to the word in the box. The words may differ in intensity or have slightly different meanings. Provide support and guidance.

4. Have students circle one word and illustrate its meaning in the base of the lamp.

## Optional

Have students demonstrate understanding of subtle variations in meaning by writing sentences using the words.

# Shades of Meaning

Some words have related meanings. For example, *whisper, talk, yell,* and *scream* all describe different ways of talking. Look at the word in the box. On the lines, list other words that have related meanings. Circle one word. Illustrate its meaning in the bottom of the lamp.

**Writing Extra!**

Use two of the words from your list in sentences. Draw pictures to match.

# Your Opinion, Please

Students demonstrate comprehension of a story by developing and supporting their own points of view about a major event.

## Preparation

Choose a book for students to read or have them choose appropriate books for their reading levels. If you'd like, choose an event from the story for students to respond to and write it in the book shape before making copies. Otherwise, students can select an event independently.

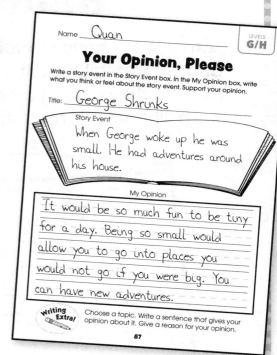

1. Have students write the book title on the line provided.

2. Direct students' attention to the event you selected, or have them think of an exciting or interesting event from the story on their own. They can record the event in the appropriate space.

3. Invite students to think about the event and form an opinion. Ask them how they feel about the event: *Do they find it funny, exciting, or sad? Do they think the character should have behaved differently? Do they like how it turned out?* Students should write their opinions in the box labeled My Opinion.

4. Challenge students to support their opinion with a reason.

## Optional

For the Writing Extra! activity, have students share their opinions on a season of the year or another topic. Remind them to give reasons for their opinions.

Name _____

# Your Opinion, Please

Write a story event in the Story Event box. In the My Opinion box, write what you think or feel about the story event. Support your opinion.

Title: _____

Story Event

My Opinion

Writing
**Extra!**

Choose a topic. Write a sentence that gives your opinion about it. Give a reason for your opinion.

# Pick a Poem

Here students explore some of the special imagery that poems use to convey meaning.

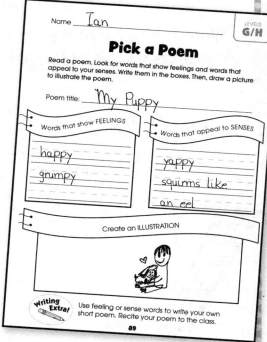

## Preparation

Choose a poem for students to read or have them choose appropriate poems for their reading levels. You may choose to read a poem aloud to the class, but be sure students have individual copies.

1. Have students write the poem's title on the line provided.

2. After reading the poem, have children look back and record any words from the poem that express feelings. Have students record the words in the box on the upper left. If students struggle with this, model using some feeling words or consider creating a list of feeling words for students to use as a reference point.

3. Have students record any words from the poem that appeal to their senses. Remind students that the five senses are sight, smell, touch, hearing, and taste. Again, extensive modeling and a reference list may be helpful. Have students record the words in the box on the upper right.

4. Encourage students to create an illustration to match the poem.

## Optional

The Writing Extra! activity challenges students to write a short poem of their own. Take time to share various types of poetry and make sure students know that not all poetry rhymes. Students may wish to write list poems, shape poems, cinquain poems or free verse. Have students recite their poems or create an audio recording.

# Pick a Poem

Read a poem. Look for words that show feelings and words that appeal to your senses. Write them in the boxes. Then, draw a picture to illustrate the poem.

Poem title: _____

### Words that show FEELINGS

### Words that appeal to SENSES

### Create an ILLUSTRATION

**Writing Extra!**

Use feeling or sense words to write your own short poem. Recite your poem to the class.

Leveled Reading-Response Activities for Guided Reading © 2013 by Rhonda Graff, Scholastic Teaching Resources

# Petal Prediction

Good readers make predictions before and during reading. They gather clues from the title, pictures, or text and draw conclusions. This activity provides great practice.

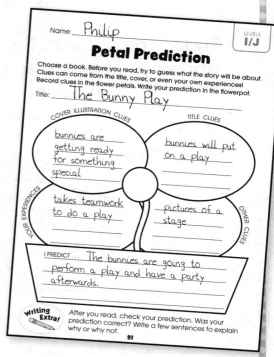

## Preparation

Choose a book for students to read or have them choose appropriate books for their reading levels. Note that this activity should be completed *before* students read.

1. Have students write the book title on the line provided.

2. Review the directions and have students notice the different kinds of clues they will be looking for to make their predictions: clues from the title, clues from the cover illustration, clues from their own experiences or knowledge (perhaps they have read other books in the series, etc.), and other kinds of clues.

3. Direct students to look for clues that help them predict what the story will be about. Have them write each clue in the appropriate petal. Let students know that they may not find all four types of clues; in some cases they may leave a petal or two blank.

4. Have students put all that information together and make a prediction. They can write it in the flowerpot using the sentence starter *I predict . . .*

## Optional

For the Writing Extra! activity, have students revisit their predictions after reading. Ask them to explain whether their predictions were correct. Let students know that authors like to surprise us; even if a prediction was incorrect, it may well have been logical.

# Petal Prediction

Choose a book. Before you read, try to guess what the story will be about.
Clues can come from the title, cover, or even your own experiences!
Record clues in the flower petals. Write your prediction in the flowerpot.

Title: _____

COVER ILLUSTRATION CLUES

TITLE CLUES

YOUR EXPERIENCES

OTHER CLUES

I PREDICT . . .

**Writing Extra!**

After you read, check your prediction. Was your prediction correct? Write a few sentences to explain why or why not.

# Trait Cap

Students use a character's actions, speech, and thoughts to identify that character's traits.

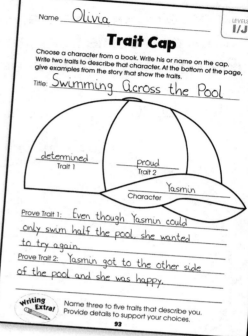

## Preparation

Choose a book for students to read or have them choose appropriate books for their reading levels.

1. Have students write the book title on the line provided.

2. Have students choose a character from the story and write the character's name on the line in the brim of the cap.

3. Encourage students to think about how the character acts, what he or she says, and how he or she thinks in the story. Have students use this information to determine a character trait for the character they chose. Write it on the cap on the line marked "Trait 1". You may wish to provide children with a list of character traits (see page 174).

4. On the line marked "Prove Trait 1," have students support their choice with specific examples from the text. They may cite actions, thoughts, or quotes.

5. Have students repeat steps 3 and 4 for second trait.

## Optional

The Writing Extra! activity challenges students to identify traits that they would use to describe themselves. Students can consult the list of traits on page 174. Have them provide details to support their choices.

Name _____

# Trait Cap

Choose a character from a book. Write his or name on the cap.
Write two traits to describe that character. At the bottom of the page,
give examples from the story that show the traits.

Title: _____

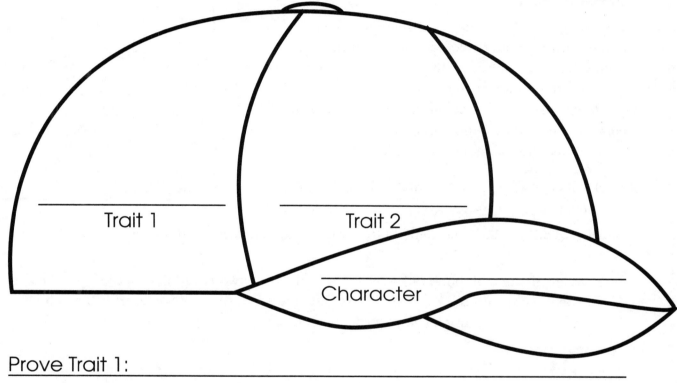

Trait 1          Trait 2

Character

Prove Trait 1: _____

_____

_____

Prove Trait 2: _____

_____

_____

Name three to five traits that describe you.
Provide details to support your choices.

**93**

# Back to the Book

In this activity, students learn to skim the story for details they may have forgotten.

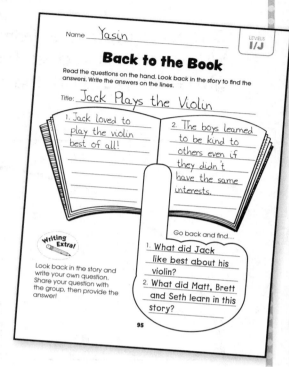

## Preparation

Choose a book for students to read or have them choose appropriate books for their reading levels. Before making copies, write two questions in the hand for the students to answer. Depending on students' abilities, the questions can be "right there" comprehension questions, inferential questions, or open-ended questions needing story support.

1. Have students write the book title on the line provided.

2. After reading, direct students' attention to the questions that you have written on the reproducible.

3. Have students look back in the story to find the answers and then write them on the book shape on the reproducible. Guide students to understand that they can skim the story looking for key words instead of rereading the entire text.

## Optional

For this Writing Extra! activity, students get to play teacher. Have students look back into the story and write their own "Go back and find . . ." question. (Have them note the answer as well.) Have the students share their questions with the group. If possible, an adult should monitor the discussion to check comprehension.

# Back to the Book

Read the questions on the hand. Look back in the story to find the answers. Write the answers on the lines.

Title: _____

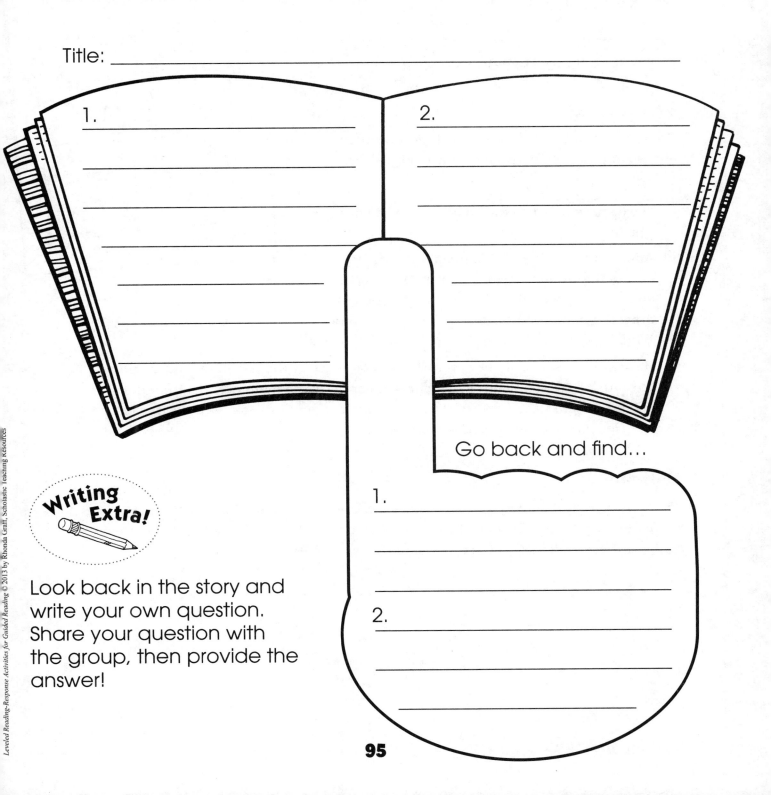

1. _____

2. _____

Go back and find...

1. _____

2. _____

**Writing Extra!**

Look back in the story and write your own question. Share your question with the group, then provide the answer!

# Beginnings and Endings

Exploring story beginnings and endings helps students better understand story structure.

## Preparation

Choose a book for students to read or have them choose appropriate books for their reading levels.

1. Have students write the book title on the line provided.

2. After reading, have students identify the key events that took place at the beginning of the story. In the box labeled "Beginning," students can write and draw the main event(s). Discuss the importance of the beginning of a story. Ask: *What information is given that helps set up the rest of the story?*

3. Have students identify key events that took place at the end of the story. In the box labeled "Ending," students can write or draw the main event(s) from the story ending. Discuss the importance of the ending of a story. Ask: *What ends are tied up? How is the action brought to a close?*

## Optional

The Writing Extra! activity gives students a chance to express their opinions. Have students tell whether they liked the story's ending and why or why not. Have them support their responses with story details.

Name _____

# Beginnings and Endings

Choose a book. At the top of the page, write and illustrate how the story begins. At the bottom of the page, write and illustrate how the story ends.

Title: _____

**Beginning** : :

```
_____
_____
_____
```

: : **Ending**

```
                    _____
                    _____
                    _____
```

Did you like the story's ending? Why or why not? Write a few sentences sharing your opinion.

# Key Events

In this activity, students recall the major events in a story, an important step in summarizing or retelling.

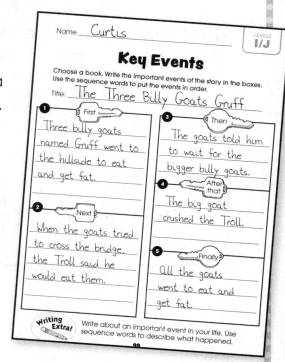

## Preparation

Choose a book for students to read or have them choose appropriate books for their reading levels.

1. Have students write the book title on the line provided.

2. Draw attention to the transition words in the boxes (*first, next, then, after that, finally*). Guide students to understand that words like these signal time order. Show that the story action will move top to bottom on the left, then top to bottom on the right.

3. Have students recall the key events from the story and write them in the boxes. Have them use the transition word in each box to move sequentially through the story. Be sure students note the story problem in one of the boxes and note how it is solved in another.

## Optional

For the Writing Extra! activity, have students write about and draw a key event in their lives. Encourage them to use sequence words to describe what took place.

# Key Events

Choose a book. Write the important events of the story in the boxes. Use the sequence words to put the events in order.

Title: _____

**1** First

_____
_____
_____
_____
_____

**2** Next

_____
_____
_____
_____
_____

**3** Then

_____
_____
_____

**4** After that

_____
_____
_____

**5** Finally

_____
_____
_____

Writing Extra!

Write about an important event in your life. Use sequence words to describe what happened.

# What's Next?

It's sequel time! In this activity, students make a prediction for a continuation of a favorite story.

## Preparation

Choose a book for students to read or have them choose appropriate books for their reading levels.

1. Have students write the book title on the line provided.

2. After reading, have students think about what could happen next to the characters. Ask: *What will the characters do now that this story is over? Will there be another adventure? Where will the characters go?* Have the students write their predictions in the balloon basket.

4. In the balloon itself, have children illustrate their predictions for a sequel.

5. Explain that some authors really do write sequels or continuations for their books. Discuss whether students have ever read a sequel or seen one in the movies.

## Optional

For the Writing Extra! activity, have students use their predictions to create a cover and title for a sequel. Have them describe why the title would be a good choice.

# What's Next?

Think about the book you just read. Predict what will happen to the characters after the story ends. Write your ideas in the balloon's basket. Illustrate your prediction in the balloon.

Title: _____

What will
happen next?

_____
_____
_____
_____

Pretend you are the author! Use your prediction to plan a second book about the same characters. Create a title and book cover for your book.

# Picture Notes

Challenge students to integrate and evaluate information presented in illustrations to help make sense of a story.

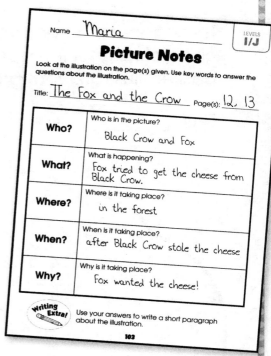

## Preparation

Choose a book for students to read or have them choose appropriate books for their reading levels. If you'd like, select an illustration for the students to observe and write the page number(s) on the reproducible before copying.

**1.** Have students write the book title on the line provided.

**2.** If you did not preselect an illustration, have students browse through the book after reading to choose an interesting picture. Have them write the page number(s) of the illustration on the line provided.

**3.** Have students read the five "W" questions and use the illustration to answer them. Students may respond in key words instead of full sentences if they wish.

## Optional

For the Writing Extra! activity, have students think about how this illustration helps tell the story. Have them use their responses to the questions to write a short paragraph about the illustration.

Name _____

# Picture Notes

Look at the illustration on the page(s) given. Use key words to answer the questions about the illustration.

Title: _____ Page(s): _____

| | |
|---|---|
| **Who?** | Who is in the picture? |
| **What?** | What is happening? |
| **Where?** | Where is it taking place? |
| **When?** | When is it taking place? |
| **Why?** | Why is it taking place? |

**Writing Extra!**

Use your answers to write a short paragraph about the illustration.

# Fish for Meaning

Use this activity to explore two different vocabulary words or one word with multiple meanings.

## Preparation

Choose a book for students to read or have them choose appropriate books for their reading levels. Before copying, fill in the two fish shapes with words you'd like students to explore. You may use a single word with multiple meanings or two different words. Words may or may not be from a book students have read. For a list of multiple-meaning words, see page 174.

1. Have students read the selected word(s).

2. If you selected one word with multiple meanings, explore another example of a multiple-meaning word to show students what is expected of them. For example, say: *A bat can be an animal that flies at night or a stick used in baseball.* Then have students think about and write the two meanings of the word you have selected. Discuss.

3. If you have selected two different words, encourage students to use their own prior knowledge, a dictionary, or context clues (if the word is from a book) to identify the meanings and write them on the lines.

4. Have students illustrate the meanings.

## Optional

The Writing Extra! activity challenges students to write their own sentence for each word. As an additional challenge, if using a multiple-meaning word, have students try to write a sentence using both meanings of the word in a single sentence.

Leveled Reading-Response Activities for Guided Reading © 2013 by Rhonda Graff, Scholastic Teaching Resources

Name _____

# Fish for Meaning

Read the word(s) in the fish. Write the meanings of the word(s) on the lines. Illustrate the meanings in the space provided.

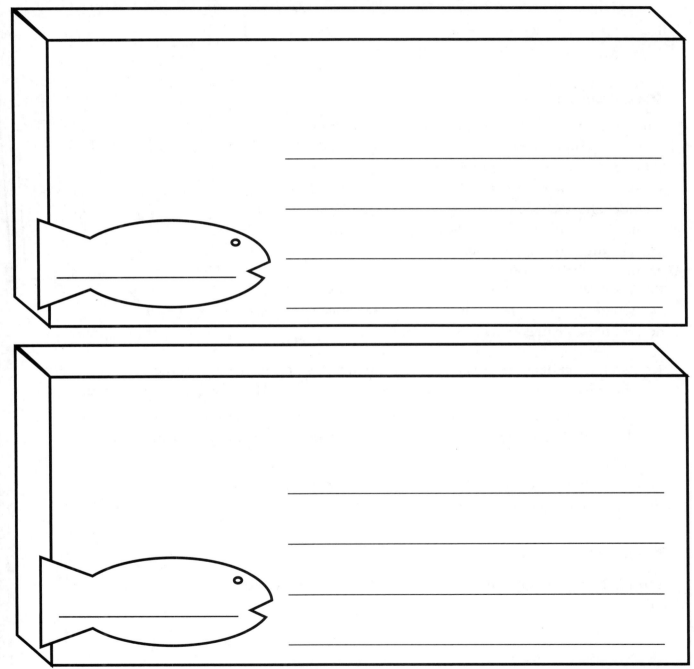

**Writing Extra!** Write your own sentences using each of the words.

# Sort It Out

With a bit of advance preparation, you can use this flexible sorting activity to explore anything from vowel sounds to character traits.

**Name** Rasha

LEVELS I/J

### Sort It Out

Look at the words in the Word Box. Use the column headings to sort them into three groups. Write each word in the column where it belongs.

Title: _____ Town Mouse and Country Mouse

**WORD BOX**

| straw bed | peas | cheese |
| owl | busy streets | loud noises |
| feather bed | wheat field | apple |

| CATEGORY | CATEGORY | CATEGORY |
| --- | --- | --- |
| City | Country | Food |
| feather bed<br>busy streets<br>loud noises | straw bed<br>owl<br>wheat field | peas<br>cheese<br>apple |

107

## Preparation

Choose a book for students to read or have them choose appropriate books for their reading levels. Preview the reproducible and decide on words you would like students to sort. Some choices for this level include: short and long vowels, words with differing numbers of syllables, or words with target digraphs. The sorting can also focus on story elements (for example, words that describe different characters). Fill in the Word Box before making copies. If you would like, you can also fill in category headings. Otherwise, students will determine the categories on their own.

1. Carefully review the directions for the activity. If you have filled in the category headings, explain that students will decide which words belong in each category.

2. If you left the headings blank, explain that students will determine categories for the words by looking at common attributes among the words. Help students get started.

3. Have students write the headings (if necessary) and write each word in the appropriate column.

## Optional

Extend the activity by having students write a few related sentences about one of the categories.

# Sort It Out

Look at the words in the Word Box. Use the column headings to sort them into three groups. Write each word in the column where it belongs.

Title: _____

## WORD BOX

_____    _____    _____

_____    _____    _____

_____    _____    _____

## CATEGORY          ## CATEGORY          ## CATEGORY

_____    _____    _____

# Two Texts

Here students analyze how two texts address similar themes or topics.

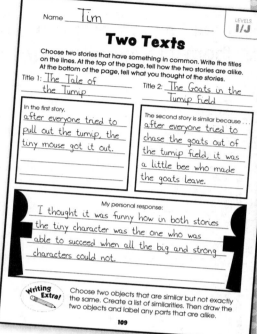

## Preparation

Choose two books for students to read or have them choose two appropriate books for their reading levels. Be sure the books have something in common, such as similar characters, settings, or problems.

1. Have students write the two book titles on the lines provided.

2. Encourage students to think of similarities between the chosen books. On the left, have them write about the common aspect from the perspective of the first story. Example: *In the first story, a boy named Joe loses his kite.*

3. On the right, have students write about the common aspect from the perspective of the second story. Example: *The second story is similar because Rachel loses her puppy in the park.*

4. Have students write a personal response. Encourage them to write how they felt, what they liked, or what they would like to change. Remind them to support their responses. Example: *It made me happy when the two characters both found what they lost. Joe found his kite in the stream. Rachel found her puppy by making posters.*

## Optional

For the Writing Extra! activity, have students choose two objects and create a list of similarities. Then, have the students draw the objects and label the parts that are alike. Some examples include: a crayon and a pencil, a notebook and a diary, a glass and a mug.

# Two Texts

Choose two stories that have something in common. Write the titles
on the lines. At the top of the page, tell how the two stories are alike.
At the bottom of the page, tell what you thought of the stories.

Title 1: _____     Title 2: _____

_____             _____

In the first story,

_____

_____

_____

_____

The second story is similar because . . .

_____

_____

_____

_____

My personal response:

_____

_____

_____

_____

Choose two objects that are similar but not exactly
the same. Create a list of similarities. Then draw the
two objects and label any parts that are alike.

Leveled Reading-Response Activities for Guided Reading © 2013 by Rhonda Graff, Scholastic Teaching Resources

# Character Close-Up

Students get to know story characters through their actions and feelings.

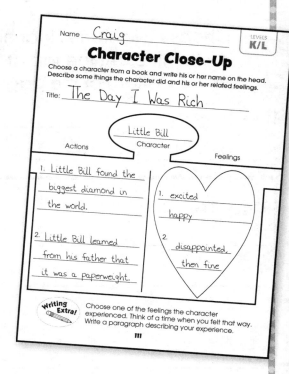

## Preparation

Choose a book for students to read or have them choose appropriate books for their reading levels.

1. Have students write the book title on the line provided.

2. Have students choose a character and write the character's name on the line in the head shape.

3. Have students think about the story and note some of the character's actions in the column on the left.

4. Invite students to think about how the character felt as a result of each action. Have them write the corresponding feelings in the heart shape on the right. For example, if the character won a race, the character might have felt happy and proud. If the character waited for a friend who never came, the character might have felt disappointed.

5. Encourage students to support their choices.

## Optional

For the Writing Extra! activity, have students choose one of the feelings the character experienced. Have them write a paragraph describing a time they felt the same way.

# Character Close-Up

Choose a character from a book and write his or her name on the head.
Describe some things the character did and his or her related feelings.

Title: _____

Character

Actions                                    Feelings

1. _____

_____

_____

2. _____

_____

_____

1. _____

_____

2. _____

_____

Choose one of the feelings the character
experienced. Think of a time when you felt that way.
Write a paragraph describing your experience.

Leveled Reading-Response Activities for Guided Reading © 2013 by Rhonda Graff, Scholastic Teaching Resources

# Character Traits

Characters' reactions to major challenges allow students to get to know the characters more in depth. That leads to better insight and understanding.

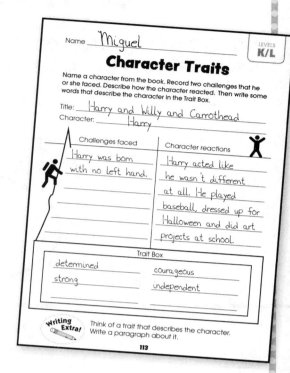

Name **Miguel**
### Character Traits

Name a character from the book. Record two challenges that he or she faced. Describe how the character reacted. Then write some words that describe the character in the Trait Box.

Title: Harry and Willy and Carrothead
Character: Harry

| Challenges faced | Character reactions |
|---|---|
| Harry was born with no left hand. | Harry acted like he wasn't different at all. He played baseball, dressed up for Halloween and did art projects at school. |

Trait Box
| | |
|---|---|
| determined | courageous |
| strong | independent |

Writing Extra! Think of a trait that describes the character. Write a paragraph about it.

113

## Preparation

Choose a book for students to read or have them choose appropriate books for their reading levels. You can also choose a character for students to focus on and write the name on the reproducible before making copies. If you worry that your students will have trouble naming character traits, you can fill in the Trait Box before making copies. (See page 174 for examples of traits.) Include a variety of traits, some of which accurately describe the character.

1. Have students write the book title on the line provided. If you did not preselect a character, have students choose a character and record the name.

2. Have students identify one or two challenges or major events faced by the character and write them in the column labeled "Challenges Faced."

3. Have students describe how the character responded to those challenges in the column labeled "Character Reactions." Responses should be specific and detailed.

4. Explain that the way people respond to challenges can tell us a lot about them. Have students use their notes about the character's reactions to select two character traits. If you have filled in the Trait Box, have students circle appropriate traits. If you have left it blank, have students write some traits that describe the character. Check that children don't confuse character traits with character feelings.

## Optional

For the Writing Extra! activity, have students write about a trait that describes the character.

# Character Traits

Name a character from the book. Record one or two challenges that he or she faced. Describe how the character reacted. Then write some words that describe the character in the Trait Box.

Title: _____

Character: _____

| Challenges Faced | Character Reactions |
|---|---|
| _____ | _____ |
| _____ | _____ |
| _____ | _____ |
| _____ | _____ |
| _____ | _____ |
| _____ | _____ |

Trait Box

_____          _____

_____          _____

_____          _____

**Writing Extra!**

Think of a trait that describes the character. Write a paragraph about it.

# Watch Me Change

Students deepen their understanding of character development by exploring how a main character changes over time.

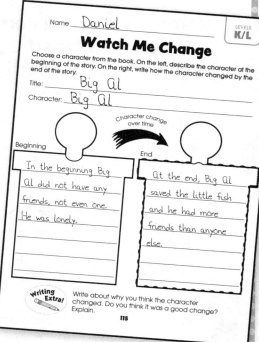

## Preparation

Choose a book for students to read or have them choose appropriate books for their reading levels. Be sure the book features a character who changes in some way through the course of the story.

1. Have students write the book title on the line provided.

2. Have them choose a character who changes in the story and write the character's name on the line. (Direct students to use main characters instead of minor characters; main characters usually change in some way while minor characters often remain static.)

3. In the character shape on the left, have students write how the character acts and feels at the beginning of the story.

4. In the character shape on the right, have students describe how the character acts and feels at the end of the story.

## Optional

Have students complete the Writing Extra! activity by explaining why they think the character changed. Do they think it was a positive change? Why or why not?

# Watch Me Change

Choose a character from the book. On the left, describe the character at the beginning of the story. On the right, write how the character changed by the end of the story.

Title: _____

Character: _____

Character change
over time

Beginning

End

Write about why you think the character changed. Do you think it was a good change? Explain.

**115**

# Question Letters

Students practice looking back in a text if they do not recall key information.

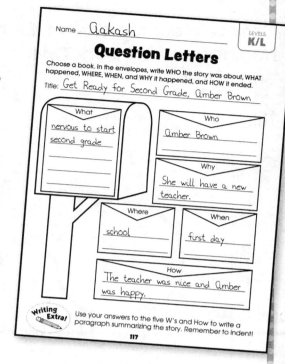

## Preparation

Choose a book for students to read or have them choose appropriate books for their reading levels.

1. Have students write the book title on the line provided.

2. Draw attention to the question words on the envelopes. Note: If students do not have experience answering the five W's and How, you may need to help them turn the words into concrete questions, such as:

   • Who are the main characters?

   • What happens?

   • When and where does it happen?

   • Why does it happen?

   • How does it end?

3. On the envelope shapes, have students briefly identify the *who, what, where, when, why* and *how* of the story. Students can respond using key words.

## Optional

For the Writing Extra! activity, have students turn their answers into a summary paragraph about the story. Be sure students know how to structure a paragraph.

# Question Letters

Choose a book. In the envelopes, write WHO the story was about, WHAT happened, WHERE, WHEN, and WHY it happened, and HOW it ended.

Title: _____

What

Who

Why

Where

When

How

Writing Extra!

Use your answers to the five W's and How to write a paragraph summarizing the story. Remember to indent!

Leveled Reading-Response Activities for Guided Reading © 2013 by Rhonda Graff, Scholastic Teaching Resources

# Story News

Read all about it! In this activity, the stories students read make headlines.

## Preparation

Choose a book for students to read or have them choose appropriate books for their reading levels. Bring in an assortment of newspapers for children to review. This will provide an opportunity for them to see how a newspaper is formatted. Be sure to point out the use of headlines, photographs, and captions.

1. Have students write the book title on the line provided.

2. Ask students to recall an important story event and create a headline for an article about the event. Explain that a headline tells the most important idea. Encourage students to be creative, because headlines should be catchy and interesting to readers.

3. For the news article beneath the headline, have students write a few sentences summarizing the event. Suggest that students try to answer *who, what, where, when* and *why*. (You will need to model summarizing many times before students really get the hang of it.) Remind students that retelling does not involve their opinions—just the facts! Let them know that newspapers have a separate place for people to share their opinions.

4. Have students draw a picture to go with the story and write a sentence (caption) explaining the picture.

## Optional

The Writing Extra! activity asks students to create a "newspaper article" highlighting an interesting event in their own lives. Encourage children to include pictures and captions.

Name _____

# Story News

Choose a book. Write a newspaper article about an interesting event from the story.

Title: _____

---

## Story News                    Edition 1 page 1

_____

Headline: _____

_____

_____

_____

_____

Picture:

Caption: _____

---

Write a newspaper article about an important event in your life. Be creative! Add a headline and draw a picture.

# Tell a Tale

Students will experience some fairy tale magic as they compare two tales or two different versions of the same tale.

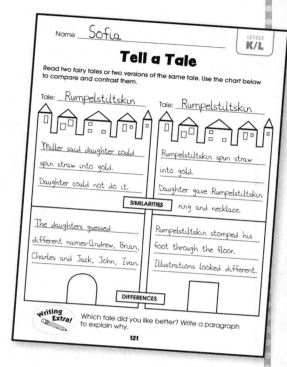

## Preparation

Find two versions of the same fairy tale for students to read. (If you have trouble finding two versions of the same one, you can easily adapt the activity to compare two different tales. The student activity page was designed to accommodate either approach.)

**1.** Have students write the fairy tale title(s) on the lines provided. Optional: You may choose to have students identify the two versions in some way (for example, by author's last name).

**2.** After reading, have students find the similarities between the books. Have them write the similarities in the tops of the two castles.

**3.** Have students think about the differences between the two tales. Write the differences in the bottoms of the two castles.

**4.** Discuss the message or moral of the story.

## Optional

For the Writing Extra! activity, invite students to decide which tale they like better. Have them write a few sentences explaining their thinking.

# Tell a Tale

Read two fairy tales or two versions of the same tale. Use the chart below to compare and contrast them.

Tale: _____        Tale: _____

SIMILARITIES

DIFFERENCES

**Writing Extra!**

Which tale did you like better? Write a paragraph to explain why.

Leveled Reading-Response Activities for Guided Reading © 2013 by Rhonda Graff, Scholastic Teaching Resources

# Which Genre?

In this book-log activity, students explore several different fiction genres.

Name _Kandi_

LEVELS
K/L

## Which Genre?

Each time you read a book, think about the genre, or group, it belongs to. Write the book title under the correct genre heading below. Under "Prove It," tell why the book fits in that genre.

| Realistic Fiction | Fairy Tale | Fantasy/Science Fiction | Fable/Folktale |
|---|---|---|---|
| New Shoes for Silvia | Jack and the Magic Harp | | |
| **Prove It!** | **Prove It!** | **Prove It!** | **Prove It!** |
| Silvia got new shoes. | Once upon a time | | |
| She kept trying them | Magic | | |
| until she grew into | Lived happily ever | | |
| them. This could | after | | |
| really happen. | | | |

**Writing Extra!** Write a paragraph explaining which genre is your favorite and why. Include details from one of the books you read.

## Preparation

Make copies of this handout for students to keep in a reading folder or book basket, since they will be returning to it several times. Start by choosing a book or having students choose a book in one of the four genres listed.

1. After reading the first book, help students decide what genre it belongs to. Have them write the title in the appropriate genre column. Remind students of the following:

   • Realistic fiction describes stories that could actually happen to real people or animals.

   • Fantasy or science fiction often focuses on made-up creatures, future worlds, or magic.

   • Fairy tales are tales in which magical things happen.

   • Fables are folktales that teach a lesson about something. They often have talking animals.

2. Have students add evidence from the book that shows it belongs to that genre.

3. Have students repeat steps 1 and 2 for other books until all the genres are completed.

4. Encourage students to share their sheets when done, as this handout will lend itself to wonderful discussion.

## Optional

The Writing Extra! activity asks students to describe which genre is their favorite, and why.

Name _____

# Which Genre?

Each time you read a book, think about the genre, or group, it belongs to. Write the book title under the correct genre heading below. Under "Prove It," tell why the book fits in that genre.

| Realistic Fiction | | Fairy Tale | Fantasy/Science Fiction | Fable/Folktale |
|---|---|---|---|---|
| | | | | |
| **Prove It!** | | **Prove It!** | **Prove It!** | **Prove It!** |
| | | | | |
| | | | | |
| | | | | |
| | | | | |

**Writing Extra!**

Write a paragraph explaining which genre is your favorite and why. Include details from one of the books you read.

*Leveled Reading-Response Activities for Guided Reading* © 2013 by Rhonda Graff, Scholastic Teaching Resources

# Support Your Response

In this versatile activity, you craft your own text-based question and students answer, supporting their responses with evidence from the text.

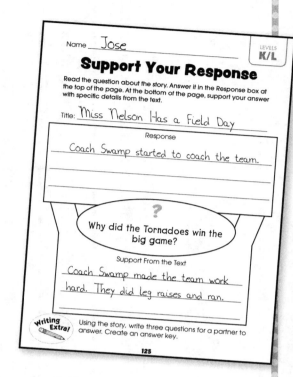

Name __Jose__

LEVELS K/L

### Support Your Response

Read the question about the story. Answer it in the Response box at the top of the page. At the bottom of the page, support your answer with specific details from the text.

Title: Miss Nelson Has a Field Day

Response

Coach Swamp started to coach the team.

?

Why did the Tornadoes win the big game?

Support From the Text

Coach Swamp made the team work hard. They did leg raises and ran.

Writing Extra!

Using the story, write three questions for a partner to answer. Create an answer key.

125

## Preparation

Choose a book for students to read or have them choose appropriate books for their reading levels. Before making copies, write a comprehension question inside the figure's head for your students to answer. The question should be inferential if possible, encouraging students to draw a conclusion and support their responses.

1. Have students write the book title on the line provided.

2. After reading, have students read the comprehension question you posed. Instruct them to answer it in the box above the figure's head. Remind students not to guess but to look back in the text for answers or clues.

3. In the figure's shirt, have students note the evidence from the text that allowed them to answer the question. Ask: *How do you know? What detail(s) in the story helped you answer the question?* If you'd like, tell students to include the page number where they found their evidence.

## Optional

For the Writing Extra! activity, have students write three story-based questions for a friend to answer. Have them create an answer sheet containing the correct responses. Have the students share their questions and check each other's answers.

Name _____

# Support Your Response

Read the question about the story. Answer it in the Response box at the top of the page. At the bottom of the page, support your answer with specific details from the text.

Title: _____

Response

_____

_____

_____

**?**

Support From the Text

_____

_____

_____

Using the story, write three questions for a partner to answer. Create an answer key.

# Rate a Story

Students get a chance to rate a book and explain their thinking.

## Preparation

Choose a book for students to read or have them choose appropriate books for their reading levels.

1. Have students write the book title on the line provided.

2. After reading, explain that students will be sharing their opinions about the book. Review that an opinion is a statement that shows how someone thinks or feels. Unlike a fact, it cannot be proved true.

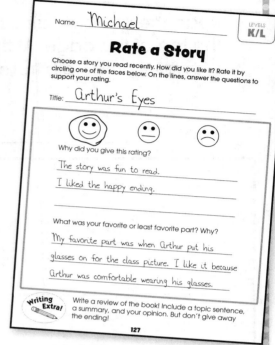

3. Have students rate the story by circling or coloring one of the faces. If necessary, explain that the face with the smile is the highest rating and the face with the frown is the lowest.

4. Have students explain their ratings on the lines provided.

5. Invite students to answer the question, *What is your favorite or least favorite part of the story?* Remind students to explain why.

## Optional

For the Writing Extra! activity, have students turn their opinions into a book review. Tell students to include an interesting topic sentence, a brief summary of story events, and their opinion. Remind students to be careful not to tell what happens at the end of the story!

# Rate a Story

Choose a story you read recently. How did you like it? Rate it by circling one of the faces below. On the lines, answer the questions to support your rating.

Title: _____

Why did you give this rating?

_____

_____

_____

What was your favorite or least favorite part? Why?

_____

_____

_____

**Writing Extra!**

Write a review of the book! Include a topic sentence, a summary, and your opinion. But don't give away the ending!

# Picturing Poetry

Explore the wonderful imagery of poetry with this activity.

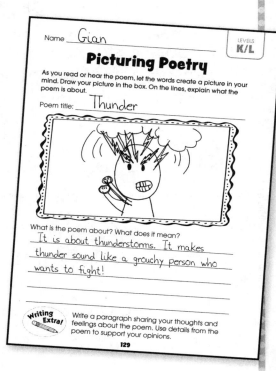

## Preparation

Choose a poem for students to read or have them choose appropriate poems for their reading levels. You may choose to read the poem aloud as students follow along.

1. Have students write the poem title on the line provided.

2. Encourage students to create a picture in their minds as they read or hear the poem.

3. In the box, have students illustrate their visualizations.

4. On the lines below the box, have children describe what the poem is about. Clarify for students that this is not a spot to share a personal opinion. Instead, students should sum up what the poem conveys. Students may need to draw conclusions from the text.

## Optional

For the Writing Extra! activity, students may write a personal response to the poem. Now they should include their thoughts and feelings. Be sure students support their opinions.

# Picturing Poetry

As you read or hear the poem, let the words create a picture in your mind. Draw your picture in the box. On the lines, explain what the poem is about.

Poem title: _____

What is the poem about? What does it mean?

_____

_____

_____

_____

_____

Write a paragraph sharing your thoughts and feelings about the poem. Use details from the poem to support your opinions.

# Dunk a Detail

Students determine the central idea of a story and identify key supporting details.

## Preparation

Choose a book for students to read or have them choose appropriate books for their reading levels. Preview the reproducible and decide which elements, if any, you want to fill in for students before copying. You can fill in the lesson and have students locate supporting details or fill in some details and have students identify the lesson. You can also let students fill in the entire page independently.

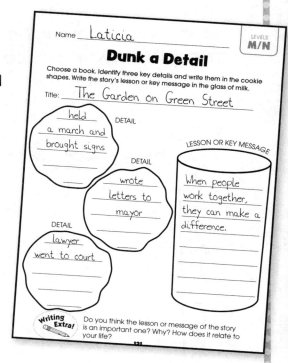

Name __Laticia__

LEVELS
M/N

**Dunk a Detail**

Choose a book. Identify three key details and write them in the cookie shapes. Write the story's lesson or key message in the glass of milk.

Title: __The Garden on Green Street__

DETAIL
held a march and brought signs

DETAIL
wrote letters to mayor

DETAIL
lawyer went to court

LESSON OR KEY MESSAGE
When people work together, they can make a difference.

Writing Extra! Do you think the lesson or message of the story is an important one? Why? How does it relate to your life?

1. Have students write the book title on the line provided.

2. In the glass shape, have students write the lesson or key message from the story (or a specific chapter). Remind students that the key message or main idea is the most important idea in the text, or the main message the author wants to get across.

3. In the cookie shapes, have students write three important details from the story or chapter that support the lesson or key message

## Optional

In the Writing Extra! activity, students are encouraged to think more about the story's lesson. Students will explain whether they think the lesson is valuable and how it might relate to their own lives.

# Dunk a Detail

Choose a book. Identify three key details and write them in the cookie shapes. Write the story's lesson or key message in the glass of milk.

Title: _____

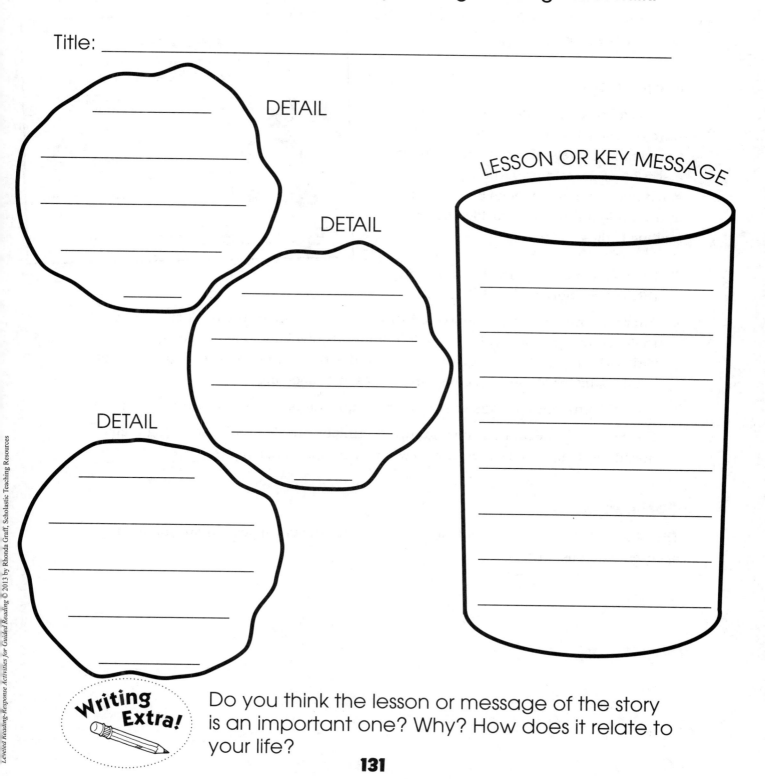

DETAIL

DETAIL

DETAIL

LESSON OR KEY MESSAGE

**Writing Extra!**

Do you think the lesson or message of the story is an important one? Why? How does it relate to your life?

# Ask About It

Students brainstorm questions about the text to discuss in small groups.

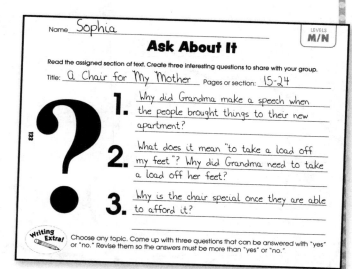

## Preparation

Choose a book for students to read or have them choose appropriate books for their reading levels. If you'd like, identify a section of the text or particular pages you'd like students to focus on. Record this information on the line provided before making copies.

1. Have students write the book title on the line provided.

2. After reading, have students record three questions about the book to share with their group. Urge students to develop thought-provoking, open-ended questions rather than questions that can be answered with a simple "yes" or "no." This can be challenging for students, so be sure to do some modeling.

3. Have the students provide answers for the questions on a separate sheet of paper.

4. Have students begin their next group meeting by sharing and discussing their questions. This will serve as a review and a comprehension check.

## Optional

The Writing Extra! activity challenges students to transform yes/no questions into open-ended questions.

LEVELS
M/N

# Ask About It

Name _____

Read the assigned section of text. Create three interesting questions to share with your group.

Title: _____

Pages or section: _____

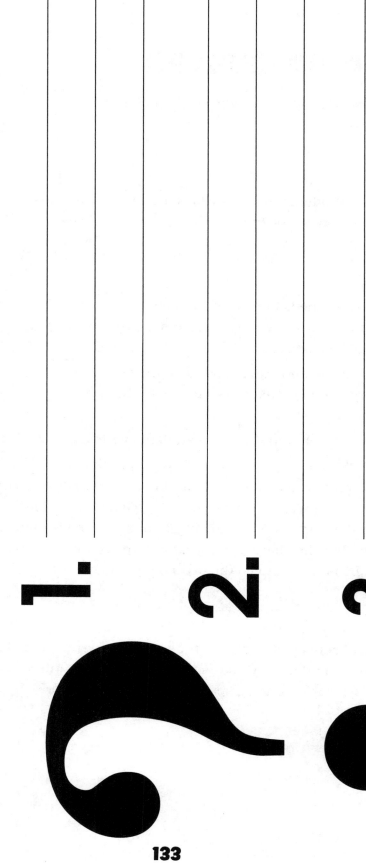

1. _____
_____

2. _____
_____

3. _____
_____

**Writing Extra!**

Choose any topic. Come up with three questions that can be answered with "yes" or "no." Revise them so the answers must be more than "yes" or "no."

*Leveled Reading-Response Activities for Guided Reading* © 2013 by Rhonda Graff, Scholastic Teaching Resources

# Character Quotes

Students analyze dialogue to learn about a main character in a story.

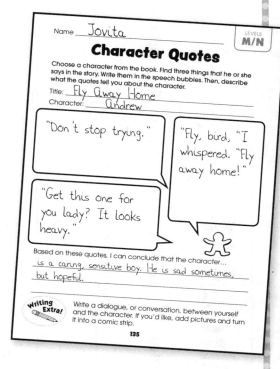

## Preparation

Choose a book for students to read or have them choose appropriate books for their reading levels.

1. Have students write the book title on the line provided.

2. Explain that dialogue is a major part of a story. It allows us to get to know the characters as we "listen" to their conversations.

3. After reading, have students choose a character from the story and write his or her name on the line provided.

4. In each of the speech bubbles, have students write a direct quote spoken by the selected character.

5. Have the students review the quotes and use them to draw a conclusion about the character. For example, if a character said, "Don't worry, Mama. I will take care of you" and "I will bring flowers to my neighbor since she is not feeling well," students can conclude that the character is kind and thoughtful. He thinks of other people's feelings and he is willing to go the extra step to help others.

## Optional

The Writing Extra! activity challenges students to try writing a dialogue of their own between themselves and a story character. If students are interested, they can turn the conversation into a cartoon using speech bubbles for dialogue.

# Character Quotes

Choose a character from the book. Find three things that he or she says in the story. Write them in the speech bubbles. Then, describe what the quotes tell you about the character.

Title: _____

Character: _____

Based on these quotes, I can conclude that the character...

_____

_____

Write a dialogue, or conversation, between yourself and the character. If you'd like, add pictures and turn it into a comic strip.

# Many Moods

Students explore how the events in a story impact the character's mood.

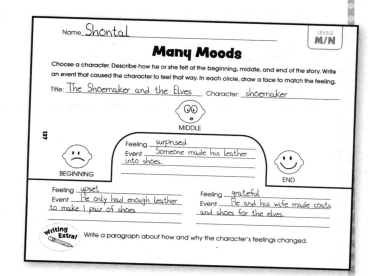

## Preparation

Choose a book for students to read or have them choose appropriate books for their reading levels.

1. Have students write the book title on the line provided.

2. After reading, have students choose a character from the story and write the character's name on the line provided.

3. Have students identify how the character felt at the beginning of the story and write the feeling on the provided line. To encourage students to think beyond "happy" and "sad," consider posting a list of "feeling" words.

4. In the blank circle, have students draw a face to match the character's feelings at the beginning of the story.

5. On the lines provided, have students describe the event that caused the character to feel that way.

6. Have students think about the character's feelings at the middle of the story. Repeat steps 3, 4, and 5.

7. Finally, have students think about the character's feelings at the end of the story. Repeat steps 3, 4, and 5.

## Optional

Have students complete the Writing Extra! activity by writing about how and why the character changed over time. Be sure they include examples from the story.

Name _____

# Many Moods

Choose a character. Describe how he or she felt at the beginning, middle, and end of the story. Write an event that caused the character to feel that way. In each circle, draw a face to match the feeling.

Title: _____

Character: _____

MIDDLE

BEGINNING

END

Feeling _____
Event _____

Feeling _____
Event _____

Feeling _____
Event _____

**Writing Extra!** Write a paragraph about how and why the character's feelings changed.

**137**

# Summary in Bloom

Students use the five W's to build summarizing skills.

## Preparation

Choose a book for students to read or have them choose appropriate books for their reading levels. Decide whether you want students to summarize the whole book or just a section. Instruct students accordingly.

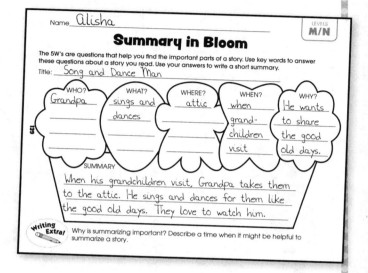

**Name** Alisha

LEVELS M/N

### Summary in Bloom

The 5W's are questions that help you find the important parts of a story. Use key words to answer these questions about a story you read. Use your answers to write a short summary.

**Title:** Song and Dance Man

WHO? Grandpa

WHAT? sings and dances

WHERE? attic

WHEN? when grand-children visit

WHY? He wants to share the good old days.

SUMMARY

When his grandchildren visit, Grandpa takes them to the attic. He sings and dances for them like the good old days. They love to watch him.

**Writing Extra!** Why is summarizing important? Describe a time when it might be helpful to summarize a story.

1. Have students write the book title on the line provided.

2. Using the whole book or the portion you preselected, have students answer the *who, what, where, when,* and *why* of the text. Note: You may need to help some students turn the words into concrete questions, such as:

   • Who are the main characters?

   • What happens?

   • When and where does it happen?

   • Why does it happen?

   Let students know it's okay to answer in key words; sentences are not necessary. If a question does not make sense for a particular story, students can leave that flower blank.

3. Have students use their answers to summarize the text in a sentence or two. Be sure to model how to summarize, as mastering this skill takes practice and time.

## Optional

For the Writing Extra! activity, have students describe when and why summarizing can be useful. In addition, have students summarize another story.

Name _____

# Summary in Bloom

The 5W's are questions that help you find the important parts of a story. Use key words to answer these questions about a story you read. Use your answers to write a short summary.

Title: _____

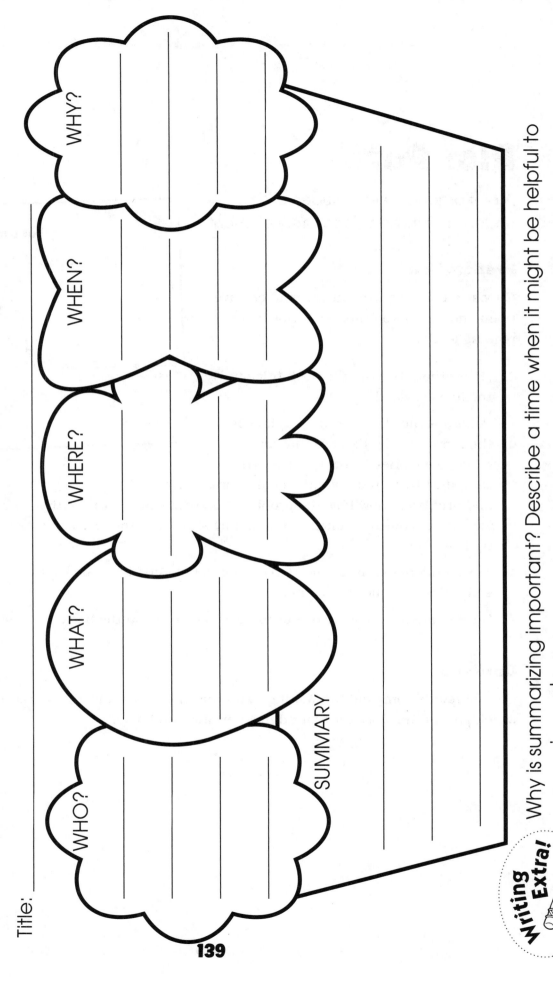

WHO?

WHAT?

WHERE?

WHEN?

WHY?

SUMMARY

**Writing Extra!** Why is summarizing important? Describe a time when it might be helpful to summarize a story.

*Leveled Reading-Response Activities for Guided Reading* © 2013 by Rhonda Graff, Scholastic Teaching Resources

# Plot Path

A plot organizer helps students understand this important story element.

## Preparation

Choose a book for students to read or have them choose appropriate books for their reading levels.

1. Have students write the book title on the line provided.

2. Point out the shape of the plot line on the reproducible. Explain that almost all simple stories follow this pattern: they start by introducing the characters, setting, and problem; show how the problem worsens, feature an exciting climax where everything comes to a head, then finally show how the problem gets solved and tie up loose ends.

3. Have students fill in the sections along the plotline to sequence the events of the story. Provide guidance as needed.

4. Have students illustrate one or more of the boxes on the back of the sheet.

## Optional

Have students complete the Writing Extra! activity by writing a paragraph detailing which part of the story they found most exciting and why.

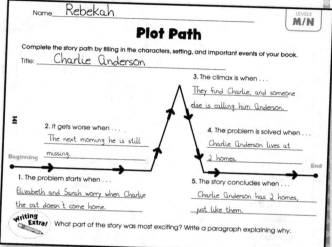

Name Rebekah

### Plot Path

Complete the story path by filling in the characters, setting, and important events of your book.

Title: Charlie Anderson

3. The climax is when . . .
They find Charlie, and someone else is calling him Anderson.

2. It gets worse when . . . .
The next morning he is still missing.

Beginning

4. The problem is solved when . . .
Charlie Anderson lives at 2 homes.

End

1. The problem starts when . . .
Elizabeth and Sarah worry when Charlie the cat doesn't come home.

5. The story concludes when . . .
Charlie Anderson has 2 homes, just like them.

Writing Extra! What part of the story was most exciting? Write a paragraph explaining why.

Name _____

# Plot Path

Complete the story path by filling in the characters, setting, and important events of your book.

Title: _____

3. The climax is when . . . .
_____
_____

4. The problem is solved when . . . .
_____
_____

5. The story concludes when . . . .
_____
_____

2. It gets worse when . . . .
_____
_____

**Beginning**

**End**

1. The problem starts when . . . .
_____
_____

**141**

**Writing Extra!** What part of the story was most exciting? Write a paragraph explaining why.

*Leveled Reading-Response Activities for Guided Reading* © 2013 by Rhonda Graff, Scholastic Teaching Resources

# Multiple Viewpoints

This activity helps students acknowledge differences between the points of view of two characters.

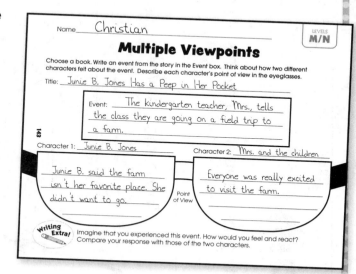

## Preparation

Choose a book for students to read or have them choose appropriate books for their reading levels. If you'd like, choose an event or situation from the story and write it in the Event box before making copies. Be sure the event involves at least two characters who see the situation differently. If you prefer, students may choose an event on their own.

1. Have students write the book title on the line provided.

2. Have students choose an event from the story if you have not already done so. This can be challenging, as the event must be perceived differently by two characters. They should describe the event in the box provided.

3. Have students select two characters who are somehow affected by the event and write their names above the eyeglass frames.

4. In the eyeglass lenses, have students write how each of the characters felt about or responded to the event. Students should recognize that each character will have a unique point of view. Discuss as a class or in small groups.

## Optional

Have students describe their own perspective on the situation for the Writing Extra! activity. Ask: *How would you feel and act if you found yourself in that situation?* Be sure students explain their thinking.

Name _____

# Multiple Viewpoints

Choose a book. Write an event from the story in the Event box. Think about how two different characters felt about the event. Describe each character's point of view in the eyeglasses.

Title: _____

Event: _____
_____
_____
_____

Character 1: _____

Character 2: _____

Point
of View

**143**

Leveled Reading-Response Activities for Guided Reading © 2013 by Rhonda Graff, Scholastic Teaching Resources

# Double Meaning

Words with multiple meanings can be problematic for some readers. Here's a fun way to clear up the confusion.

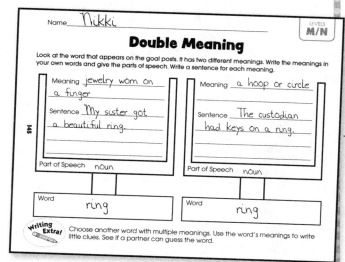

## Preparation

Choose a word with multiple meanings that students have recently encountered in a book or are likely to encounter. For a list of multiple-meaning words, see page 174. Write the word in the base of each goal post.

1. Review the definitions and usages of the word. Identify the parts of speech if this helps students to understand the different ways the word may be used. Use the word in sentences to illustrate both meanings.

2. In the first goal post, have them write one definition (in their own words), an original sentence using the word, and the part of speech.

3. Have students repeat step 2 for the second definition, filling in the second goal post.

## Optional

For the Writing Extra! activity, have students choose another multiple-meaning word and write clues using the word's meanings. They can challenge another student to guess the word. Example: *This word means something that shines, but it can also describe something that's not very heavy (light).*

Name _____

# Double Meaning

Look at the word that appears on the goal posts. It has two different meanings. Write the meanings in your own words and give the parts of speech. Write a sentence for each meaning.

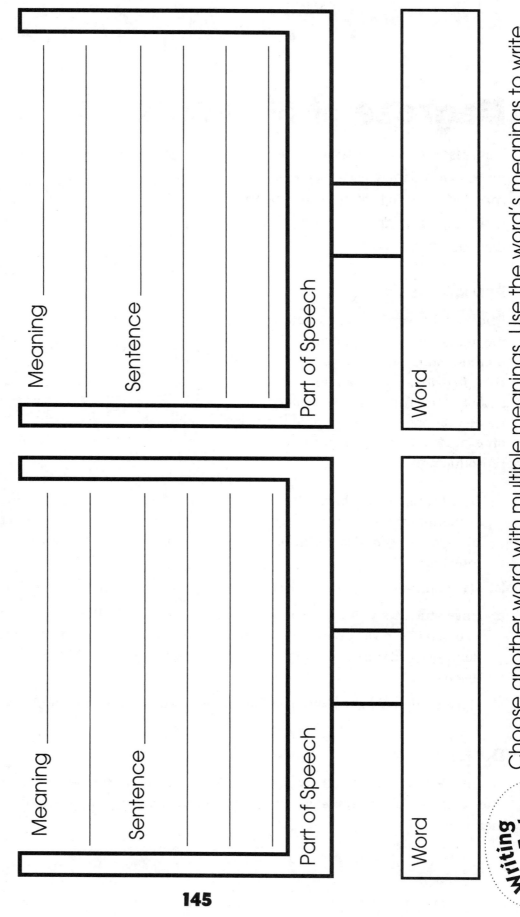

Meaning _____

_____

Sentence _____

_____

_____

Part of Speech

Word

Meaning _____

_____

Sentence _____

_____

_____

Part of Speech

Word

**Writing Extra!**

Choose another word with multiple meanings. Use the word's meanings to write little clues. See if a partner can guess the word.

# Degrees of Meaning

This lesson helps students understand words with shades or degrees of meaning—words that have related meanings but different strengths or degrees of intensity.

## Preparation

Choose four words that are related in meaning but vary in intensity. Examples include *march, walk, strut, run; cool, chilly, cold, freezing.* You may choose words from a book that students have read or use the list on page 174. Scramble the word order and write the four words on the short lines below the incline prior to reproducing.

Name __Katya__

LEVELS
M/N

### Degrees of Meaning

Think about the words *warm, hot,* and *scorching.* Their meanings are related, but they have different strengths or intensities. Read the four words on the lines below. Arrange them in order of intensity and copy the words in the boxes. Then use the words in sentences on the longer lines below.

| A. | B. | C. | D. |
|---|---|---|---|
| walk | jog | run | sprint |

walk          sprint          run          jog

The children like to walk to the park.
I jog for exercise.
He will run in the race.
My friend likes to sprint because he is a fast runner.

**Writing Extra!** Write a skit or paragraph that uses the words on the organizer. Read it for your group. Use facial expressions or body movements to convey the meanings.

1. Give examples of words with degrees of meaning. For instance, point out to students that when we describe a summer day, we might say it is *warm, hot, blazing,* or *scorching.* Point out that these words have related meanings but vary in intensity.

2. Have students read the words you have preselected and discuss the meanings.

3. Have students write the words in order of intensity in the incline boxes. Be sure to discuss the variations in meaning among words. Note that there may not be a definitive order as some words may be close in meaning. This will promote good discussion.

4. Have students write sentences using the words on the lines provided.

## Optional

For the Writing Extra! activity, have students use all of the words in a short skit. They can use facial expressions and body movements to emphasize the variations in meaning.

Name _____

# Degrees of Meaning

Think about the words *warm*, *hot*, and *scorching*. Their meanings are related, but they have different strengths or intensities. Read the four words on the lines below. Arrange them in order of intensity and copy the words in the boxes. Then use the words in sentences on the longer lines below.

A. [box]    B. [box]    C. [box]    D. [box]

_____

_____

_____

_____

**Writing Extra!** Write a skit or paragraph that uses the words on the organizer. Read it for your group. Use facial expressions or body movements to convey the meanings.

*Leveled Reading-Response Activities for Guided Reading* © 2013 by Rhonda Graff, Scholastic Teaching Resources

**147**

# Series Spotlight

Many students enjoy reading multiple books from the same series. Comparing and contrasting two books from the same series can be a lot of fun.

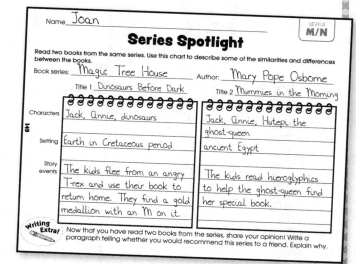

## Preparation

Choose two books from the same series for students to read or have them choose their own.

1. Have students write the series title, author, and two book titles on the lines provided.

2. Have students think about similarities and differences between the two books. Often, a series uses the same set of characters but has them experience different adventures.

3. Have students record the main characters in each book in the appropriate section. Discuss how they are alike or different.

4. Have students record the setting of each book in the appropriate section. Discuss whether the setting is the same in both books.

5. Finally, have students describe the story events of each book in the appropriate section. Students may use key words instead of sentences. Discuss any similarities or differences.

## Optional

For the Writing Extra! activity, have students write their opinion about this series. Ask students if they would recommend these books to a friend. Remind them to support their response with specific details.

Name _____

# Series Spotlight

Read two books from the same series. Use this chart to describe some of the similarities and differences between the books.

Book series: _____

Author: _____

Title 1 _____

Title 2 _____

| | | |
|---|---|---|
| Characters | | |
| Setting | | |
| Story events | | |

**Writing Extra!**

Now that you have read two books from the series, share your opinion! Write a paragraph telling whether you would recommend this series to a friend. Explain why.

**149**

# Team-Building Activities

Most of the leveled activities in this book are meant to be completed independently, although students can certainly work on them in pairs or small groups. However, the team-building activities on the pages that follow are designed as creative group projects that foster teamwork and cooperation. These activities are appropriate across all guided reading levels. You may choose the same project for multiple groups or a different project for each group. Some of the activities call for materials from your craft closet, while others revolve around the reproducibles you'll find in this section.

Remind small groups that planning and communication are important and that each student in the group should contribute to the task's completion. Realistically, children at levels A–N will need some support as they work, especially in the beginning. With practice and time, children will know what to expect when asked to work as a group.

In the Assessment section, there is a form that students can use to assess themselves after they work in a group (see page 171). This will help them learn to be self-reflective and improve their collaborative skills.

# Create a Group Mural

Students collaborate on a colorful mural celebrating a favorite story. Children will use the mural display to entice other students to read the book.

## Preparation/Materials

Each group will need scrap paper, mural paper (or multiple sheets of large construction paper taped end to end), and pencils, crayons, paint or markers.

1. Choose a book for the group to read or have students choose an appropriate book for their reading level.

2. Explain that students will be designing a mural that tells others about the story. It can depict the characters, setting, and/or important scenes from the book.

3. Provide each group with scrap paper for planning. Have the group work together using the scrap paper to plan their mural design.

4. Lay out the mural paper and supply each team with markers, crayons, or paints. Have the group use its design to create a finished product. Make sure each student gets to create a portion of his or her team's mural. If mural paper is not available, tape construction paper together to create a mural-like sheet of paper.

5. Encourage creativity as students work. If they want to make part of the mural "pop up," let them. If they want to mix different media, encourage them.

6. Have students ask the school librarian if they can hang their finished murals in the school library to promote the books . . . and teamwork!

# Make a Book Box

Students fill a box with story clues and let classmates guess the book!

## Preparation/Materials

Groups will need assorted boxes (shoe box, copier paper corrugated box, gift box), glue, paint, brushes, construction paper, crayons, markers, clay, stickers, scrap paper, and scrap materials.

1. Choose a book for the group to read or have students choose an appropriate book for their reading level.

2. Provide each group with a box. Have students paint the outside of the box so that all writing and markings are covered.

3. Have students write the title and author of the book on a piece of construction paper and put it inside the box. After presenting the box and revealing the title (Step 6), students can paste the paper to the outside of the box if they wish.

4. Have students create decorations for the outside of the box that provide clues about the story. For example, children may draw pictures of the setting, the characters, or some of the main story events. Encourage them to be creative and to think beyond the obvious.

5. Have students create or gather "props" for the inside of the box that tell more about the story. For instance, students may choose to create a character out of clay or draw an item from the story. They may also bring in small "artifacts" related to the story from home. Remind students not to bring in any valuable items.

6. Have each group present their box and let other students try to guess the book or its topic.

7. Display the book boxes.

# Big Questions

Teamwork makes investigating the five W's and H a great adventure.

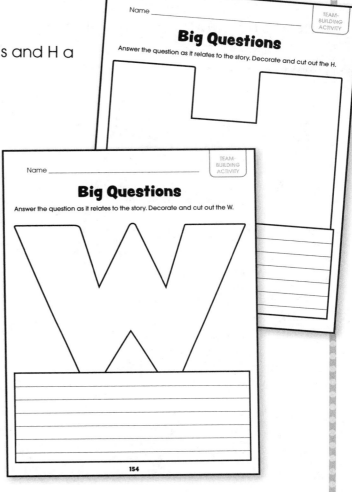

## Preparation/Materials

For each group, make five copies of page 154 (the W) and one copy of page 155 (the H). Write a different guiding question on each letter before reproducing. Some examples are listed here:

- Who is in the story?
- Who is the stronger character?
- What happened (plot/sequence)?
- Where did the story take place?
- When did the story take place?
- Why was there a problem?
- How was the problem solved?

Consider allowing students reading at higher levels to create their own questions.

1. Choose a book for the group to read or have students choose an appropriate book for their reading level.

2. Have students read the question you wrote on the first letter and discuss the answer as a group. On the lines below the letter, have them answer the question.

3. Have students repeat step 2 with the remaining five letters. They can revisit the text if needed.

4. Groups can decorate and cut out each letter (keeping their responses attached). Assemble the group's five W's and H on a large sheet of mural paper, or collate the decorated letters to create a group book.

5. Have groups use their answers to the five W's and How to create a written story summary. Encourage them to stick to the important details (no more than five to seven sentences).

# Big Questions

Answer the question as it relates to the story. Decorate and cut out the W.

# Big Questions

Answer the question as it relates to the story. Decorate and cut out the H.

# Extend the Story

Who says the ending has to be the end? In this activity, students add their own pages to a favorite book. This is an excellent extension for books with patterned, predictable text.

## Preparation/Materials

Make copies of page 157 for early reading levels. Consider using plain writing paper and drawing paper for more advanced levels.

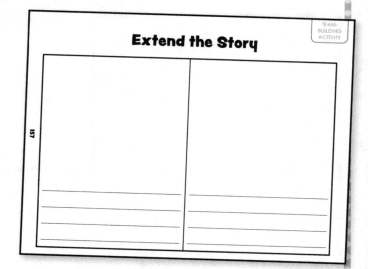

**Extend the Story**

1. Choose a book for the group to read or have students choose an appropriate book for their reading level.

2. After they've read, explain that students are going to add to the story. If using the reproducible, point out that the pages have lines for text and room for pictures.

3. If students are reading predictable, patterned text, discuss the pattern. Talk about how students can add to it. For instance, if the story pattern is "I like baseball. I like animals," a student might write, "I like ice cream" and "I like swimming."

4. If the book students read did not have patterned text, ask students what they think might happen next, after the book's ending. Have them write and illustrate their ideas on the reproducible or on plain paper.

5. Staple the group's pages together into a "book." Reread the original story aloud, adding the student-made pages.

# Extend the Story

# Puppet Play

Foster creativity and build retelling skills with a book-based puppet show!

### Preparation/Materials

Make copies of page 159 for students to use as puppet templates. You will also need wooden craft sticks to serve as handles. Optional supplies include construction paper, brown paper bags, felt, plastic "google" eyes, fabric, glue, and large boxes to turn into a puppet stage.

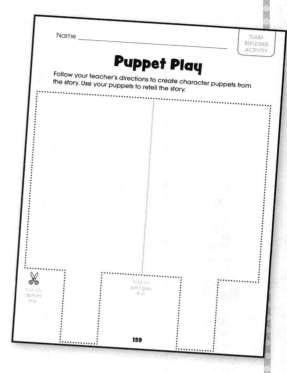

1. Choose a book for the group to read or have students choose an appropriate book for their reading level.

2. Instruct each group to create puppets for the characters in the book they read. If groups are large, students can make puppets for both main and supporting characters. Provide copies of the puppet template for students to use if they wish. Show that when the template is cut out and folded, the puppet will have both a front and back side. Students can also create their own original puppets with felt, paper, or lunch bags.

3. If students are using the template, insert a craft stick in the base as you help students fold and glue each puppet together.

4. Encourage students to create scenery for a play. They can decorate a large cardboard box or create a backdrop with pictures that reflect the story setting.

5. Consider challenging students to create a new storyline using the same characters.

6. If possible, allocate time for students to perform the play for the class or for other classes.

Name _____

# Puppet Play

Follow your teacher's directions to create character puppets from
the story. Use your puppets to retell the story.

cut on
dotted
line

fold on
solid grey
line

# Readers Theater

A Readers Theater performance based on a favorite book allows children to express creativity while honing reading skills.

## Preparation/Materials

Make copies of page 161 for students to use to plan their performance. Optional supplies include props that relate to the story or materials to make sound effects.

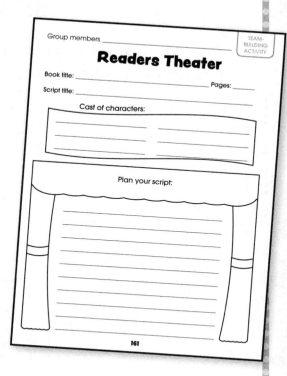

1. Choose a book for the group to read or have students choose an appropriate book for their reading level.

2. After reading, have students select a chapter or short section of the text to use for their performance. (You can assign a specific section if you'd like.)

3. Have students brainstorm a script title and write it on the planning sheet, along with the original book title.

4. Have students use the planning sheet and additional paper as needed as they work together to create a script or play of the selected scene from the book. Have them include a narrator (or two), the main character, and supporting characters. Remind them to include key information such as the setting or a summary of what happened before the Readers Theater scene takes place. This can be done through a narrator.

5. Allow time for the children to practice. Encourage them to perform for the class.

# Readers Theater

Book title: _____ Pages: _____

Script title: _____

### Cast of characters:

_____  _____

_____  _____

_____  _____

### Plan your script:

_____

_____

_____

_____

_____

_____

_____

_____

# Writing Extra! Templates

Most of the Writing Extra! activities require the students to write their responses on additional paper. The lined templates in this section can be used to provide structure and support for the early reader.

Name _____

Title _____

Name _____

*Leveled Reading-Response Activities for Guided Reading* © 2013 by Rhonda Graff, Scholastic Teaching Resources

Name

*Leveled Reading-Response Activities for Guided Reading* © 2013 by Rhonda Graff, Scholastic Teaching Resources

Name _____

# Assessment Checklists

Anecdotal notes and observations made during reading meetings can be useful for planning instruction. In this section, you will find three checklists as well as a Team-Building Self-Assessment for children to complete after collaborating on group projects. The checklists address skills on a continuum, with Checklist 1 encompassing the most basic skills (students at levels A through D). Preview the checklists before using to choose the one that best matches your students' levels and your own instructional goals.

Name _____

Comments: _____

_____

_____

| SKILL | ✓ | NOTES |
|---|---|---|
| Identifies characters | | |
| Identifies problem and solution | | |
| Identifies setting | | |
| Recalls character's actions | | |
| Makes predictions | | |
| Supports predictions | | |
| Tracks print left to right | | |
| Tracks print one to one | | |
| Recognizes and continues word pattern(s) and repetitive text | | |
| Recognizes punctuation when reading | | |
| Knows high-frequency words | | |
| Makes connections to aid in comprehension | | |
| Gathers information from illustrations | | |
| Notes similarities and differences in stories and illustrations | | |
| Retells story events in order | | |

Name _____

Comments: _____

_____

| SKILL | ✓ | NOTES |
|-------|---|-------|
| Responds to text | | |
| Determines main idea | | |
| Identifies how a character overcomes a problem | | |
| Notes character's feelings | | |
| Identifies character traits | | |
| Supports choice of character traits | | |
| Identifies cause and effect | | |
| Looks back in text for information | | |
| Retells story with details | | |
| Identifies key events | | |
| Identifies the 5 W's | | |
| Chooses favorite part | | |
| Supports choice of favorite part | | |
| Notes similarities and differences within and between texts | | |
| Responds to text through writing | | |
| Answers questions specific to a story | | |
| Provides support from text | | |
| | | |

Name _____

Comments: _____

| SKILL | ✓ | NOTES |
|---|---|---|
| Summarizes part of story or chapter | | |
| Summarizes story | | |
| Relates importance of setting to story | | |
| Poses questions about story | | |
| Differentiates facts from opinion | | |
| Provides an opinion | | |
| Supports opinion | | |
| Compares/contrasts stories | | |
| Compares/contrasts characters | | |
| Identifies genre | | |
| Recognizes character change over time | | |
| Notes interesting vocabulary | | |
| Uses new vocabulary | | |
| Draws conclusions | | |
| Uses context clues to make decisions | | |
| Connects character actions and feelings | | |
| Identifies lesson or moral | | |
| Uses dialogue to draw conclusions about characters | | |
| Notes main idea and supporting details | | |
| | | |

# Team-Building
# Self-Assessment

Team members: _____
_____
_____

Did your team finish the project?        ☐ Yes          ☐ No

What part did you complete? _____
_____
_____

Do you think that your team worked well together? Explain.
_____
_____
_____

How could your team improve?
_____
_____
_____

How do you feel about your finished project? Why?
_____
_____
_____

# Meeting the Standards

The Common Core State Standards for English Language Arts set a high bar for students to reach in their interactions with text. The activities in this book will help you and your students meet those standards. Some of the K–2 objectives covered in the activities are:

- Identify key ideas and details.

- With prompting and support, ask and answer questions.

- With prompting and support, retell familiar stories, including details.

- With prompting and support, identify characters, settings, and major events in a story.

- Ask and answer questions about key details.

- Retell stories, including key details, and demonstrate understanding of their central message or lesson.

- Describe characters, setting, and major events using key details.

- Ask and answer questions: who, what, where, when, why, and how.

- Recount stories, including fables and folktales; determine their central message, lesson or moral.

- With prompting and support, name the author and illustrator.

- Identify words or phrases that suggest feelings.

- Describe the overall structure of a story.

- Acknowledge differences in the points of view of characters, including speaking in a different voice for each character when reading dialogue aloud.

- With prompting and support, describe the relationship between illustrations and the story.

- With prompting and support, compare and contrast the adventures and experiences of characters.

- Use illustrations and details in a story to describe its characters, setting, or events.

- Compare and contrast the adventures and experiences of characters.

- Use information gained from the illustrations and words in a print text to demonstrate understanding of its characters, setting, or plot.

- Compare and contrast two or more versions of the same story by different authors or from different cultures.

- Actively engage in group reading activities with purpose and understanding.

- Ask and answer questions to demonstrate understanding of a text, referring explicitly to the text as the basis for the answers.

- Describe characters in a story (traits, motivations, or feelings) and explain how their actions contribute to the sequence of events.

- Follow words from left to right, top to bottom and page by page.

- Understand that words are separated by spaces.

- Recognize and produce rhyming words.

- Add or substitute individual sounds in simple words to make new words.

- Recognize understanding of organization and basic features of a sentence.

- Demonstrate understanding of spoken words, syllables, and sounds.

- Read common high-frequency words by sight.

- Use a combination of drawing, dictating, and writing to compose opinion pieces in which they tell a reader the topic or the name of the book and state an opinion or preference about the topic.

- Use a combination of drawing, dictating, and writing to narrate a single event or several loosely linked events; tell about the events in the order in which they occurred; and provide a reaction to what happened.

- Write narratives in which they recount two or more appropriately sequenced events, include some details regarding what happened, use temporal words to signal event order, and provide some closure.

- Write opinion pieces in which they introduce the topic or book they are writing about, state an opinion, and supply reasons that support the opinion.

- Write narratives in which they recount a well-elaborated event or short sequence of events; include details to describe actions, thoughts, and feelings; use temporal words to signal event order, and provide closure.

- Prepare for and participate effectively in a range of conversations and collaborations with diverse partners.

- Participate in collaborative conversations with diverse partners.

- Follow agreed-upon rules for discussion.

- Demonstrate command of the conventions of standard English capitalization, punctuation, and spelling when writing.

- Sort words into categories to gain a sense of the concepts the categories represent.

# Word Lists

Several activities in this book focus on character traits, multiple-meaning words, or words with "shades of meaning." If you need help getting students started on these concepts, consult the word lists below.

## Character Traits

serious, positive, cheerful, brave, angry, smart, sly, wise, stubborn, lazy, obedient, proud, helpful, foolish, brave, cautious, cooperative, dependable, dishonest, evil, friendly, greedy, responsible, nervous, trustworthy, unhappy, unfriendly, loyal, intelligent, encouraging, clever, rude, hopeful, sneaky, charming, jealous, independent, afraid, bold, thoughtful, warm, curious, giving, impatient, imaginative, easygoing

## Multiple-Meaning Words

box, pet, light, cut, check, bark, clip, play, punch, bowl, jam, sink, ring, file, bank, park, stick, stuff, bit, scale, rock, left, bat, fly, shake, trunk, back, duck, blow, hide, story, fan, well, tire, pen, rare, kind, wave

## "Shades of Meaning" Words

hot (warm, baking, sizzling), cool (cold, icy, freezing), happy (glad, excited, thrilled), big (large, giant, huge), small (miniature, tiny), mad (grumpy, upset, angry, furious), eat (nibble, munch, gobble), run (jog, sprint), look (glance, stare, peer)

# Additional Resources

Scholastic offers a host of professional books and other products to help your Guided Reading classroom run smoothly. Be sure to check these out.

## Online

http://teacher.scholastic.com/products/guidedreading

Make the Scholastic web site your first stop for the latest guided-reading research, tips on leveling, and more.

## Print

*The Next Step in Guided Reading: Focused Assessments and Targeted Lessons for Helping Every Student Become a Better Reader* by Jan Richardson.

This volume provides suggestions for preparing for guided reading as well as ideas for teaching every level, from pre-A though fluency.

*Guided Reading Fiction Focus, 2nd Edition* by Irene Fountas and Gay Su Pinnell.

This set includes a classroom library of carefully leveled fiction books, a teacher's guide, reproducible reading logs, running records, and more.

*Differentiated Small-Group Reading Lessons: Scaffolded and Engaging Lessons for Word Recognition, Fluency, and Comprehension that Help Every Reader Grow* by Margo Southall.

This research-based book helps you target reading instruction to students' specific needs.

# Notes